S0-BWM-517

The Hometown Investor

Other Books by Richard J. Maturi

THE 105 BEST INVESTMENTS FOR THE 21ST CENTURY

STOCK PICKING: THE 11 BEST TACTICS FOR BEATING THE MARKET

MAIN STREET BEATS WALL STREET

DIVINING THE DOW

MONEY MAKING INVESTMENTS YOUR BROKER DOESN'T TELL YOU ABOUT

WALL STREET WORDS

The Hometown Investor

How to Find Investment Treasures in Your Own Backyard

Richard J. Maturi

McGraw-Hill, Inc.
New York San Francisco Washington, D.C. Auckland Bogotá
Caracas Lisbon London Madrid Mexico City Milan
Montreal New Delhi San Juan Singapore
Sydney Tokyo Toronto

Library of Congress Cataloging-in-Publication Data

Maturi, Richard J.
The hometown investor : how to find investment treasures in your own backyard / Richard J. Maturi.
p. cm.
Includes index.
ISBN 0-07-040944-7
1. Investments—United States. 2. United States—Economic conditions—1993—Regional disparities. I. Title.
HG4910.M355 1996
332.6—dc20 95-23275
CIP

1 2 3 4 5 6 7 8 9 0 BKP/BKP 9 0 0 9 8 7 6 5

ISBN 0-07-040944-7

The sponsoring editor for this book was David Conti, the editing supervisor was Fred Dahl, and the production supervisor was Suzanne Rapcavage. It was set in Palatino by Inkwell Publishing Services.

Printed and bound by Quebecor/Book Press.

This book is printed on recycled, acid-free paper containing a minimum of 50 percent recycled de-inked fiber.

Dedicated in memory of our beloved Roz
1950–1994

Contents

Preface

In this age of global investing, more and more investors are searching overseas for opportunities that promise to deliver greater returns than can be found domestically. While it is wise to diversify at least a part of your portfolio in the international and global arena, don't forsake hometown investing completely at the risk of shortchanging your portfolio performance.

The Hometown Investor looks beyond the traditional realm of investing in domestic United States companies and delves into new and exciting ways to invest in your backyard. This book describes why investing in your hometown makes good economic sense and how to find value on Main Street, America.

You will learn how to ferret out unique and promising home-grown investments with substantial income and capital gains potential. You will learn how to construct a portfolio with a hometown flavor. Finally, you will become adept at recognizing Main Street investment options.

For the purpose of this book, the definition of *hometown* includes not only investment oppotunities located in your local town or city, but also those to be found in the region in which your hometown is located. To illustrate, a hometown investment for residents of my sparsely populated Wyoming might include companies or other investment opportunities in the Rocky Mountain region.

The Hometown Investor takes you from A (angels) to Z (zero coupon municipal bonds). Sit back and learn about attractive investments right under your nose.

Acknowledgments

I extend my thanks to the following who were kind enough to allow reprint of charts, illustrations, and photographs: Cambridge Development Group, National Center for Employee Ownership, and *The Red Chip Review*.

Richard J. Maturi
Cheramie, Wyoming

The Hometown Investor

PART 1

Setting the Stage

1

Hometown Investments

Like the nationally recognized expert who is taken for granted by his or her friends, hometown investments are also often neglected by local folks for a variety of reasons. To be sure, they lack the glamour and mystique of investing in foreign country or international funds. Likewise, saying that you own a part of the high-tech industry leader Microsoft Corporation has more of a ring to it than bragging to your friends about your piece of the action in the local manufacturing plant that turns out widgets day after day.

On the other hand, investors who purchased shares of another once glamorous industry leader, International Business Machines Corporation (IBM), watched the value of their shares tumble precipitously. From a 1987 high of $175⅞ per share, IBM's stock price dropped to a low of $40⅝ per share in 1993 before rebounding to the $75 per-share level in mid-February 1995, still around 40 percent of its former high stock market price.

Of course, not all hometown investments outperform their counterparts from other parts of the country or world. As with any successful investment strategy, it takes solid investigative work, thorough analysis, good timing, and a bit of luck to ferret out those hometown investments with substantial growth opportunities and the management talent to accomplish their goals.

The main point is: You should not overlook local investment opportunities in your own backyard that stand poised to deliver the kind of significant investment returns that would make Wall Street's professional money managers envious.

Microsoft Corporation and thousands of other successful firms were once small, hometown investments. In fact, Bill Gates founded his nearly $6 billion company (estimated 1995 revenues) in his garage in 1975.

Investors savvy enough to have invested in the hometown treasures found in the pages to come—before they became household names and competitors in the global economic environment—have enjoyed their participation in the growth of these firms through years of increased dividends and significant capital gains.

Hometown Investments That Have Made It Big

Microsoft Corporation
One Microsoft Way
Redmond, WA 98052-6399

Stock exchange: NASDAQ
Ticker symbol: MSFT
Telephone: 206-882-8080

As mentioned earlier, Chairman and Chief Executive Officer William H. Gates started Microsoft Corporation in his garage. The Redmond, Washington company is now the leading independent maker of personal computer software. Its trademarked Windows-based application software, such as word processing, database management, and business programs, sets the industry standard for excellence and ease of use.

The company's stock initially became public in 1986 at just over $1 per share (adjusted for two 100 percent stock dividends and three stock splits through 1994). Through fiscal year ending June 30, 1994, Microsoft completed its nineteenth consecutive year of revenue and earnings growth. The company was well on its way to its twentieth consecutive record year with fiscal 1995 earnings running more than 25 percent higher than those achieved in fiscal 1994.

The future continues to look bright. Strong new product introductions promise to allow Microsoft to garner additional market share worldwide. In addition, the company's strong financial position (no long-term debt and over $3 billion in working capital) provides the firm with substantial leverage to enter new market segments.

Hometown investors who recognized the potential of this fledgling company saw the value of their Microsoft stock skyrocket. A $1000 investment in 1986 would have been worth over $62,000 by mid-February 1995. Not a bad return on your money from a local company that started its corporate life in a garage.

Wal-Mart Stores, Inc.
Box 116
Bentonville, AR 72716

Stock exchange: NYSE
Ticker symbol: WMT
Telephone: 501-273-4000

Hometown believers saw visionary Sam Walton revolutionize the retail industry with his Wal-Mart chain. From its modest Bentonville, Arkansas roots, Wal-Mart grew to become the world's largest retailer with a chain of discount stores covering 49 states serving towns and cities with an average population of only 15,000 people. It also operates a network of Sam's Warehouse Clubs and Supercenters in metropolitan areas.

Wal-Mart is also making its presence known internationally by expanding into neighboring Canada and Mexico, with its eyes set on other emerging markets. The company has traditionally increased earnings per share in excess of 20 percent annually.

As a hometown investor, you could have purchased 100 shares of Wal-Mart Stores, Inc. stock when the company went public in 1970 at the grand price of $1650 (adjusted for stock splits). That investment would have grown to over $3.4 million when Wal-Mart's stock price peaked at $34 per share in 1993 and would still be worth over $2.4 million in mid-February 1995. In addition, Wal-Mart has paid a cash dividend every year since 1982, and Wal-Mart Directors boosted the cash dividend by nearly 33 percent in 1994.

The Home Depot
2727 Paces Ferry Road
Atlanta, GA 30339

Stock exchange: NYSE
Ticker symbol: HD
Telephone: 404-433-8211

The Home Depot represents another phenomenal success story for both the company and investors with the conviction to believe in the explosive growth possibilities of a regional building supplies/home improvement firm to expand its successful local operations and strategies to national markets.

Today, The Home Depot ranks as the home improvement industry's largest retailer with nearly 300 stores operating in 24 states stretching from the East Coast to California. The Home Depot plans to triple the number of outlets by the end of 1998 with over 800 stores in operation. The company is also making forays into the Canadian and Mexican markets with acquisitions and new store openings. Revenues and earnings continue their torrid pace with better than 20 percent increases projected for fiscal 1995 ending January 31, 1996.

From an investment perspective, The Home Depot faithful have fared well over the years, as the company grew from a small regional building supply retailer into the nation's most innovative and largest. If hometown investors saw The Home Depot's growth potential back in 1984, when the company operated only 31 stores in six Eastern seaboard states, they could have acquired a 1000-share stake in the company for around $2000 (adjusted for stock splits). In mid-February 1995, those same 1000 shares would have been worth over $50,000.

Investors could have even capitalized more by compounding their earnings by reinvesting The Home Depot cash dividends through the company's DRIP (dividend reinvestment program). The DRIP allows for the reinvestment of cash dividends, as well as the ability to purchase additional shares of company stock for cash in amounts ranging from $10 to $4000 monthly. The shareholder pays no commission charges on the stock acquisition, and the DRIP administrative expenses are absorbed by the company.

Lesser Known Hometown Investments

While these companies represent nationally and internationally recognized and respected company names, you don't have to uncover the next Microsoft or Wal-Mart to become a successful hometown investor with impressive investment returns. The following companies carry on their business in nontech, traditional industries as mundane as corrosive products and metal stamping. They operate out of what for years was known as the "Rust Belt" industrial state of Ohio. Hometown investment opportunities exist in virtually every part of the nation. As these companies demonstrate, great hometown investment opportunities exist even in the midst of an economically ravaged region such as the Rust Belt in the late seventies and eighties.

RPM, Inc.
2628 Pearl Road, P.O. Box 777
Medina, OH 44258

Stock exchange: NASDAQ
Ticker symbol: RPOW
Telephone: 216-273-5090

RPM, Inc. will be discussed in Chap. 9, but suffice it to say that Ohio area investors who saw potential in this manufacturer of industrial coatings and sealants for waterproofing and general maintenance, corrosion control, and other specialty chemical applications tracked RPM through 47 consecutive years of record revenues, earnings, and earnings per share through fiscal year ending May 31, 1994. The Medina, Ohio firm was on track to accomplish a half-century of record financial results for fiscal 1995 with both revenues and earnings up by double-digit levels over fiscal 1994 figures.

RPM has maintained a nearly 20 percent annual growth rate in earnings and dividends per share over the last decade. Over the past 24 years, the value of its shares has risen in excess of 5500 percent (assuming dividend reinvestment).

Commercial Intertech Corporation
1775 Logan Avenue
Youngstown, OH 44505

Stock exchange: NYSE
Ticker symbol: TEC
Telephone: 216-746-8011

Another Rust Belt firm illustrates how a hometown investment in an unglamorous industry can grow into one with national and international implications and significant stock gains. Local investors could purchase shares in the Youngstown, Ohio metal bender Commercial Shearing Company (later renamed Commercial Intertech Corporation) for under $6.50 per share in the early eighties. The original investment of $6500 for 1000 shares would have been worth around $20,000 in mid-February 1995. In addition, the shares would have paid out approximately $4000 in cash dividends over the past decade.

From its roots as a custom metal bender, Commercial Intertech has expanded to garner major market shares in its three business segments (hydraulic components, fluid purification systems, and metal products). It has emerged as an international corporation with 46 percent of annual revenues derived from international business. Overall, Commercial Intertech operates 36 facilities in nine countries.

In a recent coup, the company acquired two former East German hydraulic companies with no financial investment, and negotiated over $30 million in funding from Germany to make these companies viable enterprises under the Commercial Intertech corporate umbrella. The move gives the firm added hydraulic capacity and a strong foothold in the emerging Eastern European market. Not bad for a hometown investment.

Finding Value in Your Backyard

From these examples, it is obvious that intriguing hometown investment opportunities occur in every industry and location across the country. No matter where you live and work, you too can discover investment treasure not readily known to other investors outside your neck of the woods. With the exception of a few states, such as my own Wyoming, nearly every state can lay claim to at least one Fortune 500 Industrial or Fortune 500 Service company and countless undiscovered firms with great growth potential. Refer to Table 1-1 to see how your state or region ranks in terms of America's largest companies' headquarters locations.

Even if large publicly owned companies are not headquartered in your state (Wyoming has only one New York Stock Exchange listed company), they may have sales, warehousing, distribution, and plant facilities within your state's borders. To illustrate, Burlington Northern and Union Pacific maintain facilities in Wyoming, as do many large coal, oil, and natural gas corporations, not to mention utility companies, regional banks such as KeyCorp and Norwest Corporation, and other financial service companies such as Inter-Regional Financial Group (Dain Bosworth) and Piper Jaffray, Inc.

Beneath the tier of Fortune 500 Industrial and Service companies, there's an abundance of lesser known but solidly profitable publicly traded companies that could make enticing investments to enhance your portfolio without leaving your backyard. Here are some tips for uncovering promising investments:

- Seek out financially sound companies exhibiting a pattern of revenues and earnings growth backed by a strong balance sheet.
- Find businesses that you can understand and that look competent in your analysis of their prospects.
- Search for underlying, unrecognized value. Underpricing by the market due to hidden assets, new products or services, technological breakthroughs, turnaround situations in the making, and spinoff opportunities are examples.

Being close to the action on the home front gives you a significant competitive edge over other investors removed from the companies. Put this advantage to work for you earning higher investment returns.

Reading Your Local Economy

Before you plunk down your money on local or regional opportunities, you need to understand the economic forces at work that can impact the prospects for your return on an investment. Some investments prosper in certain economic environments while performing poorly in others. For example, zero coupon municipal bonds delivered significant capital gains

Table 1-1. Headquarters Locations

Rank	*Location*	*Service 500*	*Industrial 500*	*Total*
1	New York	75	43	118
2	California	50	48	98
3	Illinois	39	44	83
4	Texas	32	37	69
5	Ohio	24	42	66
6	Pennsylvania	24	29	53
7	Connecticut	18	26	44
8	New Jersey	18	24	42
9	Michigan	14	22	36
10	Massachusetts	18	14	32
10	Minnesota	14	18	32
12	Missouri	14	16	30
13	Georgia	14	13	27
14	Virginia	13	13	26
15	Florida	12	8	20
15	North Carolina	11	9	20
17	Wisconsin	8	11	19
18	Indiana	5	10	15
18	Washington	11	4	15
20	District of Columbia	8	3	11
20	Maryland	7	4	11
20	Tennessee	9	2	11
23	Alabama	5	5	10
23	Arkansas	6	4	10
25	Colorado	2	7	9
25	Oregon	4	5	9
27	Kentucky	4	3	7
27	Louisiana	4	3	7
27	Oklahoma	2	5	7
27	South Carolina	2	5	7
31	Arizona	4	2	6
31	Delaware	4	2	6
31	Kansas	4	2	6
31	Nebraska	2	4	6
31	Rhode Island	2	4	6
36	Idaho	3	2	5
37	Iowa	1	3	4
37	Utah	3	1	4
39	Hawaii	3	0	3
40	Alaska	2	0	2
40	Maine	2	0	2
42	Mississippi	1	0	1
42	New Hampshire	0	1	1
42	Puerto Rico	1	0	1
42	South Dakota	0	1	1
42	Vermont	1	0	1
42	West Virginia	0	1	1

as interest rates declined steadily from the late eighties through late 1993. However, if the Federal Reserve Board continued its fast-paced rate hikes through 1994 and early 1995, the outlook for long-term zero coupon municipal bonds would be a lot less bright.

That's why it's important to get a good feel for general trends in economic activity such as interest rates, unemployment rates, production capacity levels, and the like. You don't have to be a government economist and keep track of bushels full of economic statistics, but it does pay to beware of major trends, especially changes in direction or acceleration or deceleration of the pace. A ¾-point hike in the interest rate signals something very different from a ¼-point jump.

We'll look at some of the key indicators to follow, as well as where to obtain this valuable information. On the local economic scene, you can get a good feel for the prospects for hometown investments rather easily. The boys at the barber shop and the ladies at the beauty parlor know who got laid off and which firms are gearing up for a major expansion. This can be an early signal to economic activity on the state or national level as well, allowing you to position your portfolio for economic events not yet recognized by the financial community.

To illustrate, in my native state of Minnesota iron ore mines (now principally taconite producers) feed the steel mills of the East, which in turn feed the automobile assembly plants and other hardgoods made from steel. Now, if Henry Ford wants to produce enough vehicles to meet the projected 1996 demand, Ford will have to contract for steel many months ahead of time. In the same vein, the steel companies will have to contract for ore and other raw materials to make the steel for Ford and other automobile manufacturers. In reality, this process often takes place years in advance to prevent production disruptions. It may have to be refined as economic events unfold, but the original planning sets the wheels in motion.

Therefore, if the taconite plants in Minnesota go on a hiring and plant expansion binge in 1996, it may be an indicator that the automobile industry and other steel end-users are anticipating a boost in sales. You can find similar cause and effect relationships for industries and companies in your area.

You have to be careful to view local events through that larger perspective. The cause of the hiring spurt and plant expansions on Minnesota's Iron Range may not be due to higher sales projections after all. It may be the result of a shifting of the nation's steel producers to purchase more ore from domestic sources than from South American suppliers due to a number of factors ranging from interest rates, foreign currency changes, ore quality, labor problems, tarrifs, and tax incentives.

Key local and regional economic information that helps put the prospects for your potential investments into proper perspective includes such indicators as:

- Trends in employment/unemployment.
- Local business activity such as new business incorporations and housing starts.
- Power consumption and costs.
- Population trends.
- Upcoming labor negotiations, contracts, proposed tax regulation changes, workers compensation insurance changes.
- Commercial and industrial lease rate trends.
- Economic development activity.

Keeping in touch with your local, regional, and state economic and community development people can also pay big dividends. They have first-hand knowledge of the economic scene. They know which companies are moving into the area, which firms are expanding or cutting back, which firms just won lucrative exporting contracts, and other key economic information. After all, their job is to attract new businesses to the area and help existing businesses to operate more competitively. I know from keeping in contact with the Wyoming Department of Commerce folks that several of their goals are to attract value-added suppliers to the state to serve existing businesses, as well as to convince companies with operations within the Cowboy State to expand their existing facilities and to develop downstream manufacturing capabilities in Wyoming (as opposed to sending raw materials to other locations for processing).

For example, the Princeton, New Jersey–headquartered Church & Dwight Company, Inc. (the Arm & Hammer Baking Soda people) currently mines trona (the raw material for sodium bicarbonate among a myriad other products) in Wyoming, but they ship the raw material to other facilities for processing into baking soda, toothpaste, and other products. Should Church & Dwight decide to integrate end product manufacturing at their Wyoming facility, they could benefit from lower transportation, handling, payroll, and tax expenses—a possible significant competitive advantage in the marketplace.

Attracting new businesses can be a double-edged sword. First of all, an increase in the number of companies results in a sharing of the tax burden and lower costs for existing companies. Likewise, new local suppliers could help companies reduce their operating expenses for firms previously dependent on distant, more expensive suppliers.

On the other side of the coin, new companies could be direct competitors of existing firms, working to take market share away from them. In the same vein, new firms also compete for available qualified workers and other local resources, possibly causing a shortage and higher prices. This type of information can prove invaluable as you evaluate hometown investment candidates and their future prospects.

Other government agencies can also provide a wealth of knowledge on more of a macroeconomic level. The Employment Commission typically provides statistics on labor trends while the Wyoming Secretary of State Office tracks such things as new business incorporations and business failures.

Uncle Sam can also help you decipher the local economy. To illustrate, the Denver regional office of the U.S. Business Administration Office of Advocacy periodically publishes a business profile for the State of Wyoming, among other areas. It covers trends in population, employment, number of businesses, wage-and-salary income, exports, business incorporations, business failures, top industries, and job creation. The report also ranks the state in key areas in comparison with other states.

Trade Magazines and Other Sources of Information

Trade Magazines

Here's where a little extra reading time pays big dividends. By subscribing to a few trade industry magazines, you can keep on top of industry events before they hit the popular and financial press. Many trade magazines can be obtained for free by asking to be placed on their "comp" (complimentary subscription) list. Others are carried by local and university libraries. There's at least one magazine for every industry and industry sector and often many such publications.

Penton Publishing Company in Cleveland, Ohio makes its bread and butter publishing *Industry Week* and dozens of specialty magazines, each covering a different industry from foundries to restaurant equipment. If there's a business niche, somebody—somewhere—is publishing a magazine for it. There's probably even a trade magazine on trade magazine publishers.

Getting back to the expanding taconite plant capacity on the Iron Range, a regular reader of the steel and iron ore industry trade magazines would have known about events such as the shift from foreign suppliers to U.S. suppliers or the coming boost in steel production to meet rising automobile demand. Keeping abreast of industry happenings can help you put your local economic news into proper perspective so that you don't make the wrong investment decision based on half the facts.

Moving away from specific industry trade magazines, a wealth of information can be gleaned from magazines dealing with more generic economic development issues, such as *Area Development, Business Facilities, Expansion,* and *Plant, Sites & Parks.* All these periodically feature the economic forecast for specific industries. They also highlight economic trends and facility expansions around the country as well as covering economic activity on a state-by-state basis.

For example, the November 1994 issue of *Area Development* featured an article titled, "Food Industry Plants Blooming." The December 5, 1994 issue of *Industry Week* wrote about "A Profitable Year Ahead," with forecasts from such reputable analysts as the Wharton Econometric & Forecasting Analysis Group of Philadelphia and others. The article gave capsule reviews of several industries including automotive, semiconductors, and steel. In November 1994, *Business Facilities* looked at the electronic and electrical equipment sector in detail.

Trade Associations

Closely aligned with trade magazines are the trade associations, which publish a number of informative magazines, newsletters, and press releases. Again, they are free for the asking. Call them up and ask to be placed on their mailing list. A number of these are also published by independent research groups or consulting firms under contract.

I regularly receive *APICS Business Outlook Index,* which reviews economic growth indicators, manufacturing employment and shipments, order information, production planning, and a host of other items. (APICS stands for the American Production and Inventory Control Society, Inc.) I also receive *News from America's Research Group,* which is a press release covering the furniture industry. The December 1, 1994 headline, as an example, read "Rising Interest Rates Drive Down National Furniture Buying Index." This press release signals that it's probably not a good time to be loading up on furniture stocks or opening a new furniture store.

Search out the trade publications and trade associations serving the industries in your hometown region to keep posted on significant events in the industries you are tracking. A few minutes of reading can put you on the trail of a good investment prospect.

The University Connection

Many universities publish general economic information, detailed industry data and a wide variety of other topics. The information sources vary. Sometimes the University Press Relations or News Service Department sends out the information, while at other times individual departments publish and distribute their own publications. Contact the News Service Departments of your local and regional universities and colleges, and tell them the type of information you are requesting. They will gladly lead you to the appropriate people to get your name added to the mailing list.

The Purdue University News Service mails me a capsule summary of business story ideas each month. If one catches my eye, I call for more information or a full report on the topic. I also receive the Purdue University *Business Index* and *Service Industry News.* From UCLA's Institute of Industrial Relations come various news releases, such as the *1995 Outlook for Management,* discussing domestic and global economic trends, productivity gains, and labor costs.

Putting Your Broker to Work

Your friendly broker represents another easy and free way to keep a pulse on industries. The brokerage firms' research departments regularly publish industry outlooks that discuss the overall industry, plus prospects for specific firms. For example, a recent Salomon Brothers report discussed "Food/Beverages in the 1990s—A Global Menu for Investment Success."

If your own broker's firm does not issue research reports on a specific industry or company, ask him or her to request a copy for you from another firm, or you can call the other firm yourself. To find out the firms that cover the companies you're interested in, seek out the latest copy of *Nelson's Directory of Investment Research,* published by Nelson Publications, Port Chester, New York. In today's information age, many of the research reports or capsule comments are already available on the broker's computer and can be printed out almost instantaneously. If you have your own computer with a modem or fax machine, the report can be sent over to you within minutes of your request. Don't be shy about requesting information. After all, if you are paying full service commission rates, make sure you get your money's worth.

Full-service brokers also publish research on specific regions of the country, along with companies and other investments in those regions. Among others, Piper Jaffray publishes *Pacific Northwest Outlook, Emerging America,* and *Panorama* with coverage of Pacific Northwest economics and companies, high-growth companies targeting consumer needs for goods and services, and a broad spectrum of investment opportunities.

The Fixed Income Research Department of Kemper Securities, Inc. publishes the *Kemper Statewide Economic Trend Indicator Analysis.* The Securities Research people at A.G. Edwards & Sons, Inc. issue *Stocks by Region,* highlighting regional economic activity and interesting investment prospects.

Many brokerage firms also sponsor investment conferences at which they discuss a specific industry or investment strategy, or they invite a number of firms to make presentations to investors. A company we discuss later, Glacier Bancorp, Inc., was one of 23 banking institutions invited to talk to investors at the Montgomery Securities Second Western Financial Institutions Conference held in July 1994.

Ask your broker what online computer databases he or she can access to help you narrow down your investment choices. Some of the most useful ones include the Dow Jones News Retrieval, Zacks (earnings estimates), Bloomberg (key numbers and ratios such as cash flow), and First Call (compilation of earnings estimates).

You will find a list of regional brokerage firms from around the country in Chap. 9. Use the listing to provide you with a sound basis to begin searching out your own local and regional companies.

Other Regional Investment Information Sources

Across the country you can tap the resources of investment research analysts who specialize in certain regions, industries, market sectors, and/or securities. The following illustrate just a small portion of what is available if you do a little sleuthing.

The Red Chip Review, published by Crown Point Publishing, Inc. in Portland, Oregon, specializes in researching or analyzing small cap stocks with strong insider ownership targeted to outperform the market. For the most part, *The Red Chip Review* maintains a Western region bias to recognize and highlight market inefficiencies of stocks underfollowed by Wall Street.

"We feel it's critical to visit each of the companies we cover. It's especially important to determine first-hand the caliber of management in small companies. Management must be willing to talk to us or we won't cover the company," says Marcus W. Robins, Editor-in-Chief of *The Red Chip Review.* As indicated on Fig. 1-1, for its first full year of operation (August 4, 1993 to August 2, 1994), *The Red Chip Review* outperformed other market indexes.

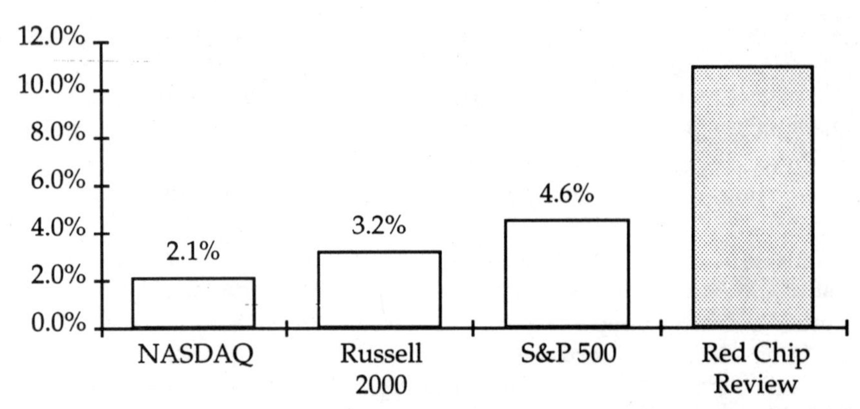

Figure 1-1. Comparison of investment returns (August 4, 1993 to August 2, 1994).

In Cleveland, Ohio, Hickory Investment Advisors, Inc. publishes *The Hickory 250.* This investment newsletter provides market commentary, updates market indexes, and highlights stocks from its universe of 250 companies in a variety of industries and market sectors, including capital goods/technology, consumer staples, basic industries, transportation, credit cyclicals, financial, and utilities.

The Hickory growth strategy portfolio is based on the following four criteria:

1. The price/earnings ratio (based on the most recent 12 months' earnings) subtracted from 100. Thus a PE of 18 would give you a score of 82.
2. The price/earnings ratio based on the median earnings of the past five years, subtracted from 100.
3. The dividend payout ratio subtracted from 100. A payout ratio of 32 would give you a score of 68. However, the maximum score for this criteria is 80.
4. The dividend payout ratio, using the median earnings, subtracted from 100. Again, 80 is the maximum score possible.

These four criteria are added and divided by 4. Scores of 81, 78, 42, and 35, for example, would give you a combined value of 59. Hickory uses all 65 Dow Stocks that are rated at least A– by the Standard & Poor's Stock Guide, plus all the Barron's 50 stocks rated at least A– as its growth portfolio universe. In the November 1994 edition of *The Hickory 250,* the following stocks had the highest growth scores:

Company	*Growth score*
McDonald's Corporation	80.10
Boeing Company	78.97
Disney, Walt Company	76.78
Raytheon Company	75.29
Hewlett-Packard Company, Inc.	74.99

Find the research and investment firms in your area and use the ones that work best for you.

Investment Clubs

Another handy source of investor information and investment-worthy companies are local investment clubs. According to data compiled by the National Association of Investors Corporation (Madison Heights, Michigan), investment clubs outperform Wall Street's professional money managers and the market averages a good percentage of the time. For a thorough discussion of investment club success strategies, profiles of successful investment clubs, and an analysis of investment club top holdings, refer to my investment book, *Main Street Beats Wall Street* (Probus, 1995).

Joining an investment club multiplies the number of people helping you perform industry and company research. Since you will, in all likelihood, come from different backgrounds and work environments, each investment club member can bring a different investment opportunity to the table. Even more important than using that information to purchase stocks for the club's portfolio, you can utilize the solid investment choices discovered through the club in your own portfolio to substantially improve those investment returns.

You can spread that information-gathering network even farther by attending regional and national investment conferences at which companies make presentations to prospective investors. Other attendees at these conferences include investment research providers such as *The Red Chip Review* and *First Call* (mentioned above).

For more information on investment clubs, contact The National Association of Investors Corporation at 711 West Thirteen Mile Road, Madison Heights, Michigan 48071, or call 810-583-6242.

Regional Mutual Funds

Mutual funds that specialize in the fortunes of regional companies are another ready source of information. Use them as a handy source list of potential investment candidates. Request a copy of their prospectuses and most recent annual or semiannual reports. These give you a summary of their investment strategies, views on the regional economy, shifts in investment sectors, and current portfolio holdings. This saves you a lot of investigative work because the funds will already have screened out the companies not positioned to do as well under their investment guidelines.

"The Midwest is in a position it has not been in since the 1950s. The region went through gut-wretching restructuring and is now positioned to reap the rewards from global demand for the products manufactured by Midwest companies," says Norman F. Klopp, Executive Vice President/Research and Fund Advisor for the Roulston Midwest Growth Fund.

Klopp also points to the diversity in the Midwest's business base ranging from autos to medical technology and from agriculture to retailing. The Roulston Midwest Growth Fund earned a 7.22 percent return for the one-year period through December 31, 1994 versus 1.3 percent for the Standard & Poor's 500 (S&P 500) Index and a 21.59 percent return from inception through December 31, 1994 versus 6.68 percent for the S&P 500 Index.

Search out your own region's undiscovered and undervalued investments for superior returns. Reading the regional fund managers' reports and keeping track of the additions and deletions to their portfolio holdings are excellent ways to seek out and monitor prospective investments in your area.

Refer to Chap. 8 for a listing of regional mutual funds and a detailed look at a number of these funds, their holdings, and their performance.

Many local and regional banks have a direct interest in the health of their local economy as well as national economic indicators. Keybank, although headquartered in Cleveland, Ohio, publishes a quarterly analysis of the Wyoming and Rocky Mountain economies. Likewise, banks such as National City Bank in Cleveland and Mark Twain Bank in St. Louis regularly issue economic forecasts. Ask your local banker to provide you with copies of their own or other banks' local and regional forecasts and reviews.

Tracking Economic Data

Economic Indicators

Indicators are measurements of the U.S. economy or securities markets that aid economists, investment analysts, and investors to understand, interpret, and predict future economic and financial events. The U.S. Department of Commerce publishes the Index of Leading Indicators (adjusted for inflation) as a forecasting tool to predict cyclical advances and declines in the nation's economy.

The Index's components are:

- Authorized housing permits.
- Average production workweek.
- Average weekly unemployment insurance claims.
- Net business investment.
- Business and consumer borrowing.
- Change in inventory levels.
- Consumer goods new orders.
- Plant and equipment orders.
- Sensitive material prices.
- Stock prices.
- Vendor performance.
- M2 money supply.

Other carefully watched indicators include total time savings deposits, brokers' cash accounts, broker margin credit, insider trading, gold prices, bond yield/prime rate ratio, stock market average price/earnings ratio, federal deficit, gross national product (GNP), and trade deficit. The financial press regularly reports on these indicators and others.

Excellent sources of business and economic data include the following:

- *Bureau of Labor Statistics,* Washington, DC: Publishes a variety of economic reports including Producer Price Indexes, Consumer Price Index, and Employment and Earnings.
- *Business Week Index,* McGraw-Hill, Inc., New York: Features capsule view of production, foreign exchange, monetary, and other economic indicators.
- *DRI/McGraw-Hill Forecasts,* DRI/McGraw-Hill, New York: Furnishes a variety of U.S. economic forecasts such as DRI Consumer Markets Forecast, DRI Current Economic Indicators, and DRI Metropolitan Area Forecast.
- *The Regional Performance Index,* The Conference Board, New York: Releases economic surveys of all regions of the country.

- *Federal Reserve Bulletins,* Federal Reserve, Washington, DC: Issues monthly publications on money and credit conditions. In addition, the individual Federal Reserve Banks publish regional and national economic reports. For example, in February 1995, the Federal Reserve Bank of Atlanta released a report stating that its production index rose substantially from December 1994 to January 1995.

Stock Indexes

A stock index reflects composite market prices for the companies comprising the index. Major stock indexes include the Dow Jones Industrial Average, Standard & Poor's 500, Value Line Index, Wilshire 500, NASDAQ Composite, Barron's Group Stock Averages, American Stock Exchange Index, and a myriad of others. More specialized indexes include the AMEX Computer Index, Daily Mutual Fund Index, Philadelphia Exchange Bank Index, Value Line Convertible Indexes, and ARMS Index (the average volume of declining issues compared to the average number of advancing issues). Stock market indexes provide a broad measurement of general or specific market sector trends.

You don't have to depend solely on these major indexes. After all, the movement of the Dow Jones Industrial Average may not accurately depict what is happening to stock prices of companies in your area. Look for local, state, and regional stock indexes released by local publishers. In Wyoming area:

- *The Omaha World Herald* publishes the Kirkpatrick Pettis Nebraska Stock Index.
- *The Boulder County Business Report* publishes both the Boulder County Stock Performance Index and the Colorado Stock Watch.
- *The Colorado Springs Business Journal* publishes the CSBJ Stock Index.
- *Colorado Business Magazine* regularly publishes lists of top Colorado public and private companies.

Other sources of corporate and industry economic data include:

- *Almanac of Business and Industrial Financial Ratios* (Englewood Cliffs, NJ: Prentice-Hall).
- *The Business One Irwin Business Almanac* (Burr Ridge, IL: Business One Irwin).
- *Forbes Annual Report on American Industry* (New York: Forbes Magazine).

- *Standard & Poor's Industry Surveys* (New York: Standard & Poor's).
- *Value Line Investment Survey* (New York: Value Line Publishing Company, Inc.).

Don't overlook your local newspaper, radio, and television media as ready sources of business and economic information. All of them have a stake in the vitality of the local economy in terms of readership and audience; they therefore have someone on staff who follows the business scene as their beat. Finally, keep in tune with the local gossip pipeline. Often company and economic news travels faster by the grapevine than through official channels as people who work at the companies, universities, and government agencies converse with their friends over a friendly cup of coffee.

Armed with all this knowledge, you are prepared to seek out value on Main Street, America and beyond. In the next chapter, we will find out how to obtain company financial and operating data and how to analyze it to find the best investment candidates.

2
Locating and Analyzing Financial and Operating Data

Knowing Your Investment

In the last chapter we discussed where to find economic and research data—the economic stage in which the companies you plan to invest must operate. Before you request financial and operating information directly from candidate companies, use your hometown advantage to good use.

Gain some first-hand knowledge about the firm. Request a tour of the company facilities. Many companies have regularly scheduled tours, while others arrange for special tours upon request. It's good public relations.

Talk to people you know who work for the company. Are they happy working for the firm? Or are they always grumbling about the inefficiency and poor labor relations? If it's a retail operation, visit the premises to see how well the store or warehouse is laid out. Note whether the employees are efficient, helpful, and pleasant.

Ask yourself the following questions:

- Is the store a nice place to shop (clean, well-lighted, convenient to traffic patterns, etc.)?
- How do the company's products compare to its major competitors in terms of quality, price, and selection?
- How do its service and warranty policies compare with industry standards?
- Would you shop here?

- Is this a company you would deal with if they had a product or service you required? (After all, if you would not buy from this company, why would anyone else?)

Companies like to maintain good relations with local business organizations. Many of their managers join groups such as the Rotary or Kiwanis Clubs. These business and service organizations are excellent places to network with top managers of these firms. If they don't belong to your club, invite them to speak about their companies and operations at an upcoming meeting.

With a good feel for the company, it's now time to zero in on the company's financial and operating information. Don't forget to perform your investment analysis fundamentals. As indicated in Chap. 1, brokerage firm research departments serve as a handy source of analysis information. Likewise, investment research sources such as Standard & Poor's tear sheets and Value Line Investment Survey (both available at many libraries) help you get a feel for the firm's past performance.

Even after you read a brokerage firm's research report on a company, it's a good idea to obtain copies of the firm's financial and operating data and review it yourself. In other words, use the research reports and investment publications as screening devices to find prospective investments.

Once you have found companies you are interested in, it's time to do some analysis work on your own. There are a number of very good reasons for doing your own research in addition to looking at research reports and other investment recommendations. First of all, different people often view the same basic financial facts differently, depending on their investment strategies. Second, a lot of company information, such as prospects for a new product or for potential market penetration, can only be analyzed subjectively, resulting in a range of equally plausible interpretations. Third, many of the brokerage firms issuing research reports provide markets for the stocks of the companies under review and may also have pending deals to underwrite upcoming security issues of the company. These events can impact an objective interpretation of the firm's future prospects. Finally, the New York-based analyst is probably not privy to information that you as a hometown investment sleuth have uncovered through close observance of the company.

Guard against becoming enamored by the local company or its management. Make an objective evaluation of the firm, its fundamentals, and future prospects in comparison with industry competitors. With that objective firmly in mind, a review of practical investment analysis and available company reports is in order.

Key Financial and Operating Reports

You have to wade through some reports to be well-versed on the company and to be able to make an informed investment decision. The reports are easy to obtain. You can request your broker to obtain copies for you (which will take a while), or you can get the name of the public relations or shareholders' relations manager for the firm under consideration and ask for the reports directly. Request to be put on the mailing list for all financial and operating reports as well as for press releases, to ensure getting timely information on important company news. A single phone call can make or save you thousands of dollars in the market.

As you analyze the financial and operating reports of potential hometown investments, make sure to compare them to other industry companies operating in regional and national markets. For example, while a local company may appear to be prospering in its local environment, exceedingly high prices may invite competition from much larger industry competitors.

Prospectus

The prospectus is a report required by the Securities and Exchange Commission (SEC); it must be given to prospective purchasers before they invest. If there is red printing on the front cover of the prospectus stating that "A registration statement has been filed but not yet become effective," you are holding a preliminary prospectus, called a *red herring* because of the red print. It indicates that the company has requested SEC permission to sell stock but has not yet received approval. Typically, the company issues the red herring about 30 days prior to the effective date (the estimated date the stock sale is expected to be approved by the SEC).

The cover will also list the estimated offering price or an estimated price range. The final price is usually set around 24 hours prior to the offering's becoming effective, based on negotiations between the company and the underwriters. The red herring serves the purpose of allowing the company to get the information out to the investing public so that investors can decide whether they have interest in an upcoming initial stock sale.

The final prospectus is printed the day the stock offering becomes effective. The red lettering is absent and the prospectus lists a firm initial price on the cover as well as a date. The issue is now ready for sale by the underwriters.

If you plan to invest in initial public offerings (IPOs), reading the prospectus thoroughly is a requirement for prudent and successful investing.

A walk through the Baby Superstore, Inc. prospectus, as an example, is instructive. The front cover does not have any red printing, indicating that it is the final prospectus and that the shares are authorized for sale by the SEC. The date of the prospectus is September 27, 1994. The initial offering price is $18 per share to the public with 2,725,000 shares contained in the offering generating $49,050,000 in gross proceeds. After the deduction of underwriting discounts and commissions totaling $1.26 per share, or $3,433,500, the balance is split between the company ($16.74 per share, or $33,320,970) and selling shareholders ($16.74, or $12,295,530). In other words, Baby Superstore will receive 73 percent of the net proceeds ($33,320,970 ÷ $45,616,500).

This is extremely important because the more capital the company has to put to work to expand, develop products, open outlets, and increase production capacity, the better the firm can position itself in the marketplace. A stock sale with the majority of net proceeds going to selling shareholders does little for the company's future prospects. In addition, if the company insiders are selling a large portion of their holdings, it raises the question about how they view the company's future.

The front cover also lists the lead underwriters, in this case CS First Boston and Invemed Associates, Inc. While not a complete endorsement of the issue, the presence of a major underwriting firm indicates that it has been convinced of the positive prospects for the underwriting and the company. After all, no underwriter wants to be associated with a market failure. Finally, the front cover lists the stock exchange on which the shares will be traded (NASDAQ) and the ticker symbol (BSST).

A word of caution: The fact that the shares have been approved for sale by the SEC in no way means that the SEC recommends them for investment. The SEC approval means only that all the i's have been dotted and the t's crossed as far as the registration process is concerned. All the required information is contained within the prospectus, but it is up to the investor to properly analyze the data.

The back page contains a Table of Contents. You can use this to refer immediately to certain sections that will help you determine faster whether the company is of interest to you as an investment. There's no need to wade through the whole prospectus if you don't like the information provided in the selected financial or the discussion of management experience. However, before you invest, read all the sections to make sure you don't miss any important facts concerning the company and its operations.

We won't discuss every page here but will hit the highlights and what to look for in certain sections. You can see from following the Baby Superstore's Table of Contents the gamut of topics covered in the prospectus.

Table of Contents

Page 2 may provide some basic information on the company. Baby Superstore uses a foldout to show the locations of the company's 41 existing locations and target locations for 1995. The prospectus also contains photos of a typical store and product lines carried.

On page 3 you get into the meat of the prospectus. The Company section provides a summary of the company's business, with more detail under the Business section. Baby Superstore is a leading retailer of baby and young children's products. It gives the scope of the firm's operations (41 stores), its strategy (a broad assortment of quality products at everyday low prices), and some basic history of the firm (when it started up, its growth experience, expansion strategy, etc.).

Next comes a description of the offering and some summary financial and operating data. Again, more detailed financial information appears in the Selected Financial Data segment later in the prospectus.

Starting on page 5, you can evaluate the Investment Considerations of the issue pertaining to the company: its business, markets, competitors, etc. This is where you need to assess the investment risks associated with the offering. For example:

- Are Baby Superstore's expansion plans too aggressive for the company's existing financial structure?

- Will the company's existing management information system and distribution network adequately handle the planned expansion?
- Is there too heavy a reliance on major suppliers and third-party contractors?
- Are the firm's revenues too dependent on one sector of the country, which may devastate earnings with the onset of a regional economic contraction?
- Is the company's success tied to one or two key personnel?

These are the types of questions you need to evaluate as you make your way through the prospectus.

Pay particular attention to the Use of Proceeds information. How will the proceeds be used to improve the company's market position and long-term performance? Dilution is also a concern that needs to be addressed. The Capitalization section illustrates the degree of leverage management plans to use. Higher leverage can mean more bottom-line per-share earnings but carries with it additional expenses (interest), which must be covered by operating earnings and therefore a higher risk posture in certain economic environments. Compare the debt/equity ratio to see if it is in line with industry standards.

Of course, studying the financial performance of the company in terms of revenues, earnings trends, and key financial ratios is of prime importance. This is discussed in detail later in this chapter (see Annual Report/Related Reports Analysis). Pay attention to financial statement footnotes. That's often where the most important information lies hidden.

Another section filled with key information is Management's Discussion and Analysis. Management outlines the company's overall business strategy and how the firm has performed in the past with a year-by-year comparison covering several periods. It discusses changes in performance and the reasons for them. It also provides a review of liquidity and the capital resources available to achieve the company's expansion goals.

The pages on the Company's Business reveal key factors in the firm's operating environment pertinent to running the business, such as:

- The industry outlook.
- Major competitors.
- Business strategy.
- Expansion strategy.
- Products and services.
- Key personnel.

- Plant and office facilities.
- Suppliers.
- Distribution.
- Information systems.
- Marketing.

It's a good idea to compare the discussion of the industry outlook and market prospects of one company's management with that of other industry companies to detect any glaring discrepancies in their visions of the future.

Now it's management's turn to be under the microscope. Does the management team possess sufficient industry and business experience to efficiently run an operation of the size they are planning? Often, technical geniuses start companies only to flounder because they do not have the personal expertise to manage. Therefore, it's important to look at the support staff of vice presidents and other officers backing up the chief executive and chief operating officers. Also look for industry and financial expertise that company management can draw on from the board of directors.

Here again is where you can put your local knowledge to effective use. Scour the names of the board members for people you know and whose judgment or reputation you value. Upstanding local citizens will hesitate to serve on the board of directors of companies that they feel possess poor prospects. In speaking with these members, indicate that you saw their names listed as board members for XYZ Corporation and ask why they decided to join that firm's board. That will usually lead to an honest discussion of the firm's potential. Also ask if their experiences on the board have met their expectations. This question could lead to very revealing information—either positive or negative.

The Principal and Selling Shareholders section reflects how much of their stake in the company major shareholders are disposing of in the initial public offering. While Baby Superstore officers and directors disposed of nearly 410,000 shares in the offering, it represented a small portion of their total holdings (less than 5½ percent), and they would still own over 60 percent of the outstanding shares of common stock after the completion of the public offering. To be sure, Baby Superstore's management and directors hold a significant part of the company, and their direct financial interests are very much tied to the success of the company. That's a good sign for prospective investors.

Your local perspective also gives you insight into why some insiders may be selling company shares. They may need to fund their child's college education or may have just purchased a new vacation home.

As mentioned earlier, it's important to know the caliber and market clout of the lead underwriters. It's also critical to know how the underwriting is being executed. You might encounter several types of underwriting. The phrase *best efforts* means that the underwriter will make a best effort to sell the issue. If the underwriting firm falls short of a sellout, the company does not get all the money it expected from the offering. Best efforts offerings place the risk on the company issuing the stock.

A *firm commitment* underwriting binds the underwriter either to sell all the shares or to purchase them in the event a sellout does not occur. Often a number of underwriting firms form a syndicate to sell an issue. That way, no one firm is obligated to purchase all the remaining unsold shares. In other words, each firm takes a piece of the underwriting action and the risk.

As indicated in the prospectus, the underwriting agreement for Baby Superstore obligates the underwriters to purchase all the offering shares, split 50/50 between the firms. Many smaller offerings may be taken on as a best efforts underwriting. If the underwriting firm is unwilling to make a firm commitment, it can mean one or more of several things:

- The firm may not like the company's prospects.
- The market for issues may not be very favorable.
- The underwriting firm may be limited by current available capital resources and the number of other deals it has already committed to.

Other underwriting terms to be on the alert for include minimax and all-or-none. Under *minimax,* the issuer accepts a minimum amount of money from the offering but is willing to accept more (up to the maximum). The phrase *all-or-none* indicates that the entire offering must be subscribed to or the issue will be cancelled.

If you sign up to purchase shares of a minimax offering and the minimum level is not reached, your shares will not be purchased despite tying up your available capital for a period of time. On the other hand, another question arises if the minimum is reached and the sale of those shares is accomplished: Are the net proceeds due the company from the less-than-maximum issue enough to accomplish the company's goals for the proceeds?

There's a lot to decipher in reading a prospectus, but it is time and energy well spent. It can help you discover companies truly capable of delivering substantial investment returns and steer you away from those that could have disastrous results for your portfolio.

Keeping in touch with your local or regional brokerage firm can help you get a feel for how well the offering is being received by the investment community, not only locally but also nationally. Broadly based interest is generally a good sign for the company's future prospects.

Analyzing a Company's Numbers

What can you determine from an analysis of the financial statements and accompanying footnotes? Up front, make sure that the company's financial statements are not subject to any conditions by the certified public accountants who reviewed the reports. CPAs don't give out conditional statements lightly and they usually spell big trouble looming for the company. In some cases, a company that issues a conditional auditing report may have its very existence threatened by factors giving rise to the conditional report. Also, companies don't change CPAs very often; so a change in accounting firms may be a signal about potential problems areas not readily observable by a quick review of the annual report. Dig deep for the facts about any accounting firm change.

A "clean" report should include language in the Independent Auditor's Report similar to the following:

> In our opinion, such consolidated financial statements present fairly, in all material respects, the financial position of XYZ Corporation and subsidiaries as of December 31, 1994 and 1993, and the results of their operations and their cash flows for each of the three years in the period ended December 31, 1994, in conformity with generally accepted accounting principles.

The Income Statement

Now move to the numbers themselves. Are the company's revenues and earnings growing? Has the growth rate been maintained, or is it tapering off or starting to decline? With your view of the industry, competitors, and potential (international?) markets, you can estimate whether the company can sustain its growth rate over the next five years.

Concentrate on the trend in operating earnings, being wary of accounting adjustments and extraordinary items that have kept earnings afloat the past few years. Keep tabs on gross margin percentages to see if there has been any slippage over the past few years. Monitor overhead to determine whether the company is still running lean and mean—or getting bloated with extra staff.

Track major key expenses from year to year to make sure management is not jockeying expenses to prop up the bottom line. For example, management could reduce research and development efforts or postpone needed equipment repair and maintenance, just to boost the bottom line for the year. But shortsighted actions like that only come back to haunt the company and your investment in later years, as the company either loses market share due to a lack of new product introductions or experiences loss of productivity and costly equipment breakdowns.

The Balance Sheet and Ratios

The balance sheet deserves as much attention as the income statement. Is the company highly leveraged and susceptible to an economic contraction? Is the company using its cash resources wisely to grow the company, or are they languishing in money market accounts? Read the footnotes on long-term debt. How does the interest rate the company is paying compare with rates paid by other firms in the industry? The rates charged by financial institutions and the financial markets reflect the degree of risk in lending to the company. A high rate acts as an early warning signal to dig deeper.

The company's *current ratio* (current assets ÷ current liabilities) indicates how well it can pay upcoming current obligations out of current assets, thereby avoiding additional debt. Other easy-to-apply liquidity gauges include the *quick ratio* [current assets – inventory ÷ current liabilities] and *working capital* (current assets – current liabilities).

Net cash flow and *cash flow per share* are also excellent indicators that the company will be able to finance operations, expansion, capital expenditures, principal and interest obligations, and dividend payments out of operating cash flow. The statement of cash flows shows how the company generates cash and how it is putting it to use. Face it, cash is king. Given two companies that are basically the same operationally, the company with the better cash flow outperforms the other company because it is able to take care of market opportunities, such as acquisitions, product development, or new markets. Companies with less cash either have to forgo such opportunities or borrow funds to take advantage of them; they operate at a competitive disadvantage due to the higher costs resulting from interest charges.

The New York Stock Exchange identifies seven key ratios that, when applied to a firm's financial statement, can give an analyst or investor clues about a company's efficiency, liquidity, and profitability:

1. Current ratio
2. Quick ratio
3. Capitalization ratio
4. Operating profit ratio
5. Sales to net fixed assets
6. Net income to net worth
7. Cost of goods sold to inventory

Tracking these ratios over time (trend analysis) can help pinpoint where the company is headed.

Ratios are important but they don't tell you a lot by themselves. They need to be interpreted in relation to other ratios. Is the debt/equity ratio increasing or decreasing? How does it compare to other companies of similar size in the same industry? Trends and relationships tell the story, helping you foresee where this company is headed and the degree of risk in its strategy.

For an excellent source of comparative historical financial data and financial ratios for a wide variety of industries and size groupings, consult the current edition of *RMA Annual Statement Studies* (Philadelphia: Robert Morris Associates). The RMA publication lists the following ratios for the industries covered:

- Liquidity ratios.
- Cost of sales.
- Coverage (dividend and interest).
- Leverage.
- Operating.
- Expense to sales.

Within each ratio category, a number of separate ratios are designed to reflect specific financial information. The front of *RMA Annual Statement Studies* describes each of the 16 ratios it uses for comparison and shows each ratio formula. It also provides industry trend data for a five-year period and a directory of other sources of composite financial data for more than 225 industry classifications.

Baby Superstore's industry category, infants' clothing retailing (SIC #5641), shows a median current ratio of 1.8 for all size firms, while the median debt to net worth ratio is 2.4 for firms with revenues up to $500,000 and 1.2 for firms over $500,000 in sales. Gross profit comes in at 36 percent for the smaller firms and over 40 percent for the larger firms. A decline of Baby Superstore's gross margin over the past few years from, say, 38 percent to under 32 percent would be a large warning sign that the company is at a major disadvantage, compared to other large industry companies, and that it is losing ground. Incidentally, Baby Superstore's gross margin is just fine.

I also recommend the following comprehensive books on financial formulas and financial statement analysis techniques:

- Robert P. Vichas, *Handbook of Financial Mathematics, Formulas, and Tables* (Englewood Cliffs, NJ: Prentice-Hall).
- Gerald I. White, Ashwinpaul C. Sondhi, and Dov Fried, *The Analysis and Use of Financial Statements* (New York: John Wiley & Sons).
- Martin S. Fridson, *Financial Statement Analysis* (New York: John Wiley & Sons).

Ask to be put on the company's mailing list for press releases to keep you appraised of ongoing happenings at the firm that may have an impact on the value of your shares.

Price/Earnings Ratio Formulas

During your evaluation process, you also have to take into consideration how the market is valuing the company. Even if the firm's projected revenues and earnings are on track for solid growth, the stock market may have that information already factored into the firm's stock price, leaving little room for further upward moves. That's where price/earnings (P/E) ratios come in handy.

Evaluating the level of a company's P/E ratio represents one way to compare its potential against alternative investments. The P/E ratio is calculated by dividing the price of a share of stock by the issuing company's earnings per share. To illustrate, if a stock sells for $30 per share and the company currently earns $3 per share, its P/E ratio is calculated as follows:

$$
\begin{aligned}
P/E &= SP/EPS \\
&= 30/3 \\
&= 10
\end{aligned}
$$

where: SP = stock price
EPS = earnings per share

The P/E ratio indicates investors' belief in the company's future earnings growth potential. The higher the P/E, the faster investors anticipate the company will grow over the next few years. Conversely, low P/E ratios indicate that investors expect lower growth or even stagnation for the company.

Analysts and investors use several different methods to calculate P/Es. The *current P/E ratio* is calculated by adding a company's reported earnings for the past six months to analysts' estimates for the next six months and dividing that sum into the company's current price per share.

The *trailing P/E ratio* is calculated by dividing the total of the past four quarters' earnings per share into the current stock price. This method eliminates the need for estimates and their related inaccuracies, but it uses historic data which may not be applicable to the future. On the other extreme and more forward-looking, the *projected P/E ratio* divides the sum of analysts' estimates for the next four quarters' earnings per share into the stock's current price.

Companies in different industries sport different P/E ratios. P/Es for a single company can also vary widely depending on the economic cycle and the overall market level. Therefore, it's important to compare a stock's current P/E ratio with those of its industry peer group, with its own historical P/E, and with the current and historic P/Es of the market, designated as the P/E ratio of the average stocks in the S&P 500 Index.

To see where the company stands in relation to the market or industry benchmark P/E, divide the company's P/E by the market or industry P/E. For example, if the market P/E is calculated at 14 and the company's P/E stands at 19, the company's relative P/E is 1.357 (19 ÷ 14). In other words, the company's growth is valued at a level more than 35 percent higher than the industry average. That's quite a divergence from the industry norm, and your analysis must decipher whether that great a premium is justified in light of the company's underlying fundamentals and prospects for the future.

Since 1953, the average market bottom P/E ratio comes out to a tad under 11, with lows of 7.0 in 1974, 8.0 in 1978, 7.6 in 1982, 8.9 in 1984, and 11.5 in 1987. Generally, market P/E ratios in excess of 20 are considered unsustainable for long periods, signaling a possible retracement.

The tools you need to put these valuable ratios to work for you in uncovering top investment candidates and undervalued situations are right at your finger tips. Your local or university library should have such resources as *Value Line Investment Survey, Standard & Poor's Stock Guide, The Wall Street Journal, Barron's,* and company tear sheets. In today's information age, there's a multitude of investment software packages to aid you in your analysis. Use these resources to your best advantage.

Put all this information and analysis together and then determine if it jibes with what you are witnessing first-hand. Do the financial reports show brisk sales growth while you observe idle workers at the loading docks of the company's facility in your area? Is management talking about expanding its line of stores while you observe empty customer parking lots outside their existing stores? Or are the stores in your area bustling with activity while the company's stock price is languishing or falling due to overall negative economic or industry bad news? This could be an opportunity to pick up the company's stock cheap.

Related Reports

Like the prospectus, the annual report and accompanying reports are packed with must-read information. The Investors' Relations or Shareholders Services Department can ship these reports to you free of cost. Also, keep in mind that a growing number of companies provide telephone update service on the company's current revenues and earnings. The appropriate telephone number will be listed near the end of the company's annual or quarterly report.

Hand in hand with the annual report review, you need to be looking at the SEC-mandated *Form 10-K,* which provides more in-depth information about the company's business, operations, management team, and financial and operating performance. Likewise, the quarterly report has its sister companion, *Form 10-Q,* with more detailed information. Also of interest to investors is the annual *Proxy Statement* and *Form 8-K,* which must be filed whenever material events such as an acquisition or takeover attempt occurs. The Proxy Statement/Notice of Annual Meeting of Shareholders alerts the investor to key issues that are going to be voted on at the annual shareholders' meeting, such as:

- The election of a Board of Directors.
- The confirmation of or a change in the company's certified public accountant (red flag).
- Proposed changes to stock option or bonus plans (possibly unwarranted corporate officer benefits).
- Authorization to amend the company's articles of incorporation to increase the number of authorized shares of common stock (potential dilution looming).

Its Security and Ownership sections also alerts you to changes in large holdings that may not have appeared elsewhere in company literature.

The annual report, backed by the Form 10-K, packs much the same type of information contained in the prospectus relating to business, industry, competition, management, management discussion, markets, marketing, government regulation, and so on. We need not repeat that discussion.

Shareholder Meetings

Being a local or regional investor gives you yet another decided advantage over more distant shareholders by allowing you to easily attend the annual shareholders meeting. This provides an excellent opportunity to question management about its strategies, new products, market expansion, past blunders, and a host of other items of importance to investors. It also provides the chance to observe management first-hand to see how they handle themselves and how good a grasp they have of operations. As a bonus, some companies such as RPM, Inc. in Medina, Ohio, hand out samples of company products to shareholders.

3

Ferreting out Hot Regions/ Hot Industries

Economic Cycles Present Opportunities

In the late seventies and through part of the eighties, Wyoming enjoyed a boom economy with heavy oil exploration activity and uranium production. Then came the bust.

Today, the economic mix is quite different. In the early nineties, Wyoming led the nation in percentage growth of new incorporations, and its limited liability laws and low taxes are generating additional interest in the state. The Cowboy State leads the nation in trona production (the raw material used in industrial processes from glass to plastics and consumer products from Arm & Hammer baking soda to toothpaste). It ranks as one of the country's top coal producers, and sports a growing and vibrant tourism industry. Similarly, throughout most of the eighties, California was *the* hot spot to be located. That was before an onslaught of problems (higher taxes, stricter business regulations, dramatic cuts in defense-related employment, earthquakes and fires) sent both companies and people fleeing its borders to nearby safer havens such as Colorado, Idaho, Oregon, Utah, and Wyoming. Today, there appears to be a glimmer of turnaround hope on the California horizon.

No matter what region of the country you live in, it is subject to economic cycles. Just as you may have to adjust your portfolio with different types of investments to respond to changes in the economic environment and maintain proper diversification, you may also have to adjust your geographical mix for the same reasons or at least shift to other industries within your local region. In investment, as in business, you have to adjust with the economic times in order to maximize your return. Don't be blindsided with devotion to your home region and industry. Face economic reality and make the necessary adjustments to safeguard the value of your portfolio.

A region's economic downturn, while causing difficulties, can present unique opportunities for smart, patient investors. In the eighties other energy and "oil patch" states, such as Colorado, Oklahoma, and Texas, saw commercial, industrial, and residential real estate prices tumble, while defaults skyrocketed, in the wake of the oil bust. The skylines of Denver, Dallas, and Houston were painfully punctuated with "see-throughs," office towers left uncompleted by bankrupted developers. Likewise, many workers fled those states, leaving behind their keys in their financial institutions' drop boxes and defaulting on their mortgages. It was simply easier and cheaper to move away and find a job elsewhere.

Any fool can make money during an economic boom. It takes investment acumen, a contrarian type of foresight, and fortitude to plunk down your money when all others are fleeing. But you could have scooped up valuable properties for a fraction of their replacement cost, and reaped significant rewards when the economies of those cities and states rebounded in the nineties. As they say, "Every cloud has a silver lining." Search for it and then act accordingly. When others are bailing out, search for value.

As Sir John Templeton says, "When others are panicking and stampeding to get out, I'm more than happy to accommodate them." Of course, Templeton has already performed his investigative work and recognizes a bargain when he sees it.

Hot and Not-So-Hot Regions

As mentioned earlier, there's plenty of resources to tap into when evaluating a region's prospects. Use these to add to your personal observations about your own region. In addition to the national press, which frequently highlights robust economies around the country, keep up-to-date on your local and regional business reading for a closer interpretation of the region's economic vitality. While the national business and financial press gives good coverage of regional events, it is not in the front trenches. More often than not, it provides follow-up articles to stories already covered by local and regional publications.

For example, *Crain's Cleveland Business, Colorado Magazine,* and *Florida Business* regard the local economies and companies as their main beat. They know what is happening way before the national press picks up on it. This is probably even more true today as many of the larger news organizations, such as *The Wall Street Journal,* have reduced the number of their regional bureaus and depend more on independent "stringers" (those working for local newspapers and other publications) to feed in local stories with a national angle.

In the same vein, keeping tabs on regional outlook research reports by local and regional brokerage firms can help keep you ahead of the curve in seeking out hot regions and hot industries to investigate for investment opportunities. For the most part, local and regional analysts are in more day-to-day contact than their counterparts on Wall Street and therefore should provide more timely and more in-depth coverage.

National economic activity statistics mask the vast differences among the performances of the regional economies. According to the U.S. Department of Labor, nonfarm payrolls for the period May 1993–May 1994 ranged from a positive 7.4 percent in Nevada to a minus 2.2 percent in Hawaii. Next door to Nevada, California suffered a minus 0.5 percent decline in nonfarm payrolls. The Rocky Mountain states showed the greatest gains along with some Southeast states, while those in decline or exhibiting the slowest growth were California, Hawaii, and a number of Northeastern states.

Regional statistics can also cover up differences in the conditions of state economies. As shown in Fig. 3-1, Alabama's nonfarm payroll grew by only 1.3 percent while surrounded by states with nonfarm payroll growth ranging from a respectible 3.0 percent (Tennessee) to a robust 5.0 percent rise (Georgia). Table 3-1 illustrates another indication of a region or state's vitality with the growth in average annual percent change in personal income for the fastest and slowest growing states. With that in mind, the following regional economic snapshots provide some fertile ground to begin your search.

Northeast/Mid-Atlantic Region

A bastion of old-line manufacturing companies, the Mid-Atlantic region is in the throes of reinventing itself to meet the challenges of the twenty-first century, with its increased global competition and reduced trade barriers. Regional chemical companies have been retrenching with associated employee cutbacks, which should pay off down the road with leaner, more efficient operations and competitive postures. Area defense con-

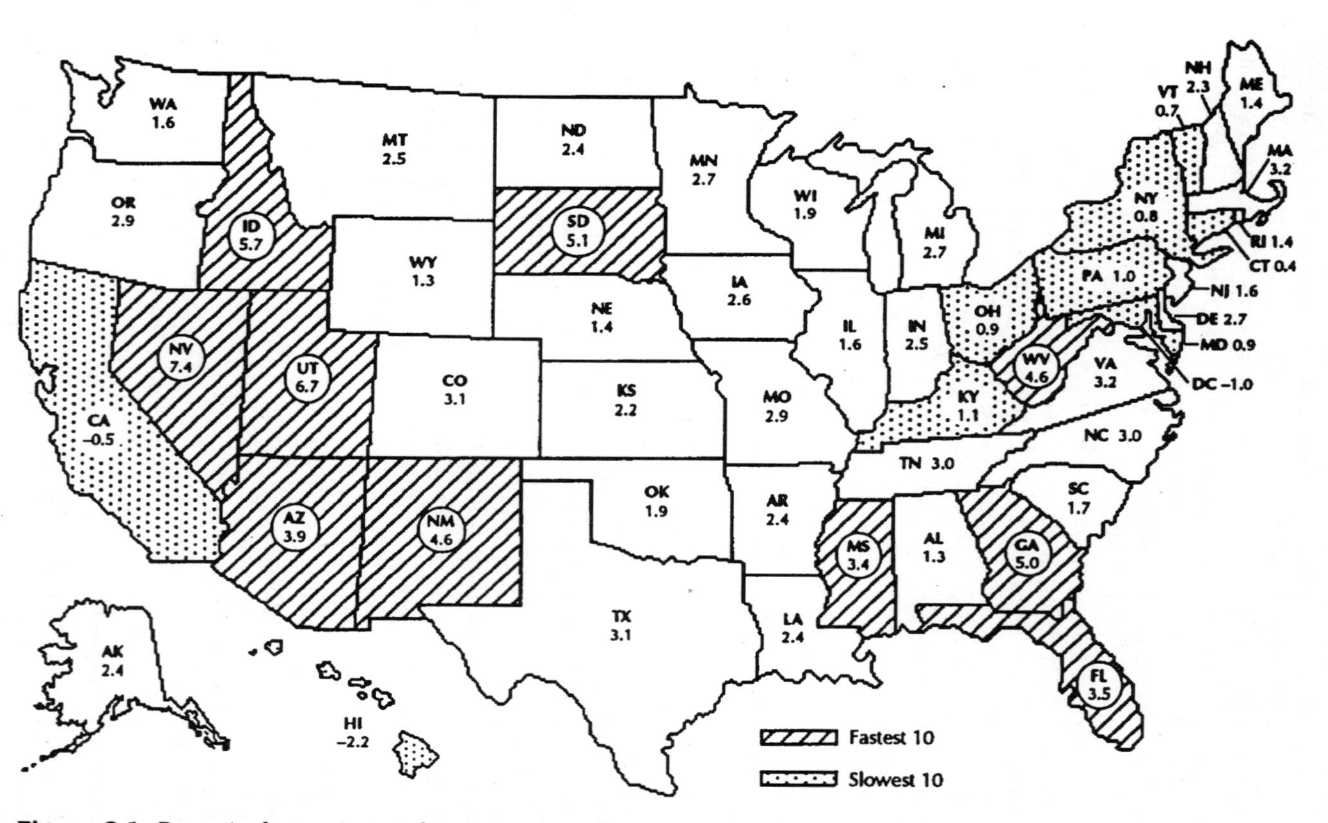

Figure 3-1. Percent change in employment on nonfarm payrolls by state (May 1993–May 1994). (SOURCE: *U.S. Department of Labor.*)

Table 3-1. Average Annual Percent Change in Personal Income (First Quarter 1991–First Quarter 1994; U.S. Average: 5.3%)

Fastest Growing States		*Slowest Growing States*	
Idaho	8.9%	California	3.0%
Nevada	8.8	Rhode Island	3.8
Utah	7.6	Maine	4.1
New Mexico	7.5	Delaware	4.2
Colorado	7.3	Massachusetts	4.2
Tennessee	7.3	Hawaii	4.3
North Carolina	7.1	Maryland	4.4
Montana	7.0	Connecticut	4.5
Arizona	6.9	Pennsylvania	4.7
Georgia	6.8	Iowa	4.8
Texas	6.8	New York	4.8

tractors have also been hard hit by cutbacks in the nation's defense budget, and pharmaceutical companies have been plagued by dramatic changes and intensified competition in the health care industry.

In many respects, this region is in a position similar to that of the Midwest's Rust Belt states in the eighties. Northeast/Mid-Atlantic states and localities are beginning to revamp their business tax and regulation strategies, and embark on innovative economic development activities to attract new business, retain existing business, and rejuvenate their economies.

On the corporate front, companies are reengineering how they conduct their business, even rethinking which business lines they should continue to pursue or which new business endeavors make sense for them in the new world competitive environment.

But all is not doom and gloom in this region. Global companies such as PepsiCo and Westinghouse still provide plenty of upside potential. There are also some unique niche companies such as Connecticut's Forschner Group, Inc. (the exclusive distributor for the Victorinox Swiss Army knife and an expanding product line) and Delaware's MBNA Corporation (the leading issuer of affinity cards and the second largest U.S. bank card lender). And don't count the old-line companies out. They are old-line companies because they have adjusted to new economic realities over the decades and survived with a renewed focus and thrust. The worst is over for this region; look for a rebound.

Southeast Region

Most of the Southeast has exhibited good employment and personal income growth in recent years, benefiting from population shifts and business relocations. Service and financial sector growth has been strong and manufacturing has been making a regional comeback, despite pockets of continued recession or slow economic growth in states like Maryland and Florida. Virginia is a mixed bag, hit by defense cutbacks affecting both the Tidewater region (Norfolk, Hampton, and Newport News) and Washington, DC metropolitan area. But new strides in the Richmond area to transform itself into a major biomedical/biotechnology center hold great promise for the future.

Even with Maryland's economic woes, it is headquarters for McCormick & Company, Inc., the world's largest manufacturer of spice and seasoning products. I featured McCormick in my book, *The 105 Best Investments for the 21st Century* (McGraw-Hill, 1995). Other Southeast companies that deserve a look include The Home Depot, Inc. (building supplies) in Georgia and Barnett Banks, Inc. in Florida. The region is also benefiting from a nationwide home-building boomlet and strong automobile demand.

Midwest/Great Lakes Region

As noted by Roulston Midwest Growth Fund's Norm Klopp, the Midwest stands to benefit from international trade as world economies demand the automobiles, machine tools, and heavy industrial products the region is noted for producing in bulk. In addition, in the shadow of the huge manufacturing giants, high-technology plastics, office equipment, and medical supply companies have sprung up throughout this region in the past decade.

Illinois' Deere & Company supplies the world's breadbaskets as the largest manufacturer of agricultural equipment, as well as industrial and lawn care equipment. Milwaukee, Wisconsin's Harley-Davidson, Inc. and Skokie, Illinois' Brunswick Corporation keep plenty busy pumping out quality products for the recreational and leisure markets. The Midwest/Great Lakes region is embarking on a robust economy not seen since the birth of the consumer economy in the early 1950s. It is home to solid, conservative banking institutions such as Banc One Corporation and KeyCorp.

Michigan's Haworth, Inc. and Cleveland's Office Max are both enjoying the consolidation of the office equipment and office supplies industry segments, with increasing demand for their products.

Central Region

Anchored by an agricultural economy on the rebound from the 1993 floods, the Central region also possesses a number of other major industries and strengths. Solid, conservative banks like Norwest Corporation benefit from a sound regional economy. The area also has a number of automotive plants that are running at nearly full capacity. The financial, insurance, business services, as well as the health industry sectors, are also performing well. Two trouble spots stem from layoffs in the defense industry and cutbacks at IBM in Rochester, Minnesota.

Expanding in reaction to increased consumer spending and the growing trend to dine out, Wichita, Kansas' Lone Star Steakhouse & Saloon boosted revenues over 180 percent in 1993. Across the border in Missouri, Emerson Electric Company has achieved 36 consecutive years of earnings per share growth and 37 years of annual cash dividend increases. With a rebound in store for the electrical equipment industry, look for stronger performances from Emerson Electric and other leading industry firms. In the insurance sector, Central region property-casualty insurers such as The St. Paul Companies (St. Paul, Minnesota) are favored with a large capital base and well-diversified product mix.

South Central Region

This region stands to derive tremendous benefit from increased trade opportunities as a result of the North American Free Trade Agreement (NAFTA), but it is still hampered by low oil and natural gas prices. Texas has shifted from a predominantly oil-driven economy to one more balanced with a large concentration of new businesses in high-tech areas such as computer manufacturing, computer software, and telecommunications. Along similar lines, Oklahoma has attracted new businesses in the service sector to replace lost oil– and natural-gas–related jobs.

Fort Worth, Texas–based Burlington Northern, Inc. looks to be a solid winner with increased NAFTA shipments and the railroads' stronger competitive position against the beleaguered trucking industry. New Orleans' First Commerce Corporation will benefit from increased economic activity in the region.

Mountain Region

By far the strongest region in the nation, the Mountain states have attracted businesses from West Coast states seeking to flee high taxes and harsh business climates. As a result, the area is enjoying a building boom as people flock to fill both new and relocated job opportunities.

Gaming's refocus to include family entertainment and to regain market share from the explosion of Nevada-based gambling operations across the country has also fueled construction activity and job opportunities in

Nevada. Utah's robust economy continues to grow with high-tech start-up ventures. In South Dakota, Gateway 2000 employs over 3100 people, and the new arrival of some Citicorp operations will keep that regional economy humming.

Montana's timber industry has been aided by the building strength in pockets around the country. The prospects for several Mountain state companies such as Glacier Bancorp, Plum Creek Timber Company, L.P., and Zions Bancorporation are discussed in detail elsewhere in this book.

Pacific/West Coast/ Northwest Region

For the most part, California has drawn much attention with disaster after disaster befalling the state. Conflicting reports show the state either emerging from its economic recession or still on the brink of yet another disaster ready to send it back into economic oblivion. Either way, there are still investment opportunities in this vast state.

The economic waves in both California and Japan have sent a rip tide through Hawaii's economy by slashing tourism visits from both regions, a major blow to the Aloha state. The major Pacific bright spot is Washington with its relatively low business costs, high quality of life, and receptive business climate. With the exception of cutbacks at Boeing Company, the rest of the state appears very healthy and likely to stay that way.

Remember, fund managers of regional funds make their living correctly analyzing their regional economies and the industries and companies within their region. Use the efforts of their research departments to get a lead on the direction of your regional economy and investment prospects. Many of these regional funds publish newsletters in addition to the required semiannual and annual reports. For example, The Roulston & Company family of funds publishes *The Steady Investor,* an investment newsletter covering such topics as dollar cost averaging, a description of the funds' portfolio results, discussions on the regional economy, and steps to make your investing simpler and better. Ask your regional mutual fund to place you on their investment newsletter mailing list.

National and regional accounting and consulting firms represent another excellent source of regional and national economic information. Companies in your area are often clients of these firms. They have a good grasp of what is happening locally, and can give that information an added national perspective. To illustrate, a recent issue of Chicago-based Grant Thornton's *Tax & Business Advisor* newsletter presented a barometer of regional expectations in terms of sales, employees, and profits, derived from data supplied from Dun & Bradstreet Information Services. The same issue also discussed the rebounding national economy and its impact on business expectations. Many times you can get on the distribution lists free for the asking.

Hot Industries

It's important to know the condition and prospects of the major industries operating in your region before you commit funds to a hometown investment. While Wyoming may be the largest uranium producer in the nation, the lack of demand for uranium in the wake of the nuclear power industry collapse makes uranium mining ventures a poor investment choice.

Seek out the industries that operate within your region and analyze their potential from both a local and national perspective (as already discussed). *Fortune* and *Business Week* periodically list top companies and industries, classified by region. In addition, the regional business publications such as *Colorado Magazine* and *Crain's Cleveland Business* regularly rank area companies in terms of criteria such as earnings growth, revenues, number of employees, number of facilities, etc. *Investor's Business Daily* lists industry groups with the greatest stocks making new highs. It also presents a table itemizing nearly 200 industry indices by such factors as earnings per share ranking, relative strength ranking, sales as a percentage of growth rate, and the industry group index. Use these lists as a starting point for discovering or confirming trends and uncovering treasure in your back yard.

The following industries are ones to watch as the national and global economies rebound. Seek out companies in your region that can compete head to head with other firms in these well positioned industries. Don't forget to keep a pulse on changing economic, technological, and political factors that can transform a dormant industry (like uranium) into a vibrant industry once again.

Chemicals

The chemical industry is on the verge of a prolonged cyclical rebound, especially if the international economic expansion gets underway in 1995 and beyond. Look for companies that have successfully restructured and are now running lean and mean. Solid chemical companies from around the country include DuPont (Wilmington, Delaware), Great Lakes Chemical (West Lafayette, Indiana), Morton International (Chicago, Illinois), and Georgia Gulf Corporation (Atlanta, Georgia). Many of these companies, although headquartered in one part of the country, operate many facilities throughout the nation and abroad.

Regional Superbanks

Industry consolidation pushed by market share, cross-product marketing, and gained efficiencies will make super-regionals out of some well positioned and capitalized banks. To the list of Banc One (Columbus, Ohio), KeyCorp (Cleveland, Ohio), and Norwest (Minneapolis, Minnesota) add the likes of NationsBank (Charlotte, North Carolina), Signet (Richmond, Virginia), First Union (Charlotte, North Carolina), and Bank of Boston (Boston, Massachusetts).

Transportation

The onset of increased trade with Mexico and Canada through NAFTA and heavier demand for Western coal due to environmental concerns will spur rail traffic over and beyond the next decade. A European rebound and greater trade with the China and the Far East will boost container ship operator revenues. Burlington Northern (Fort Worth, Texas), CSX Corporation (Richmond, Virginia), Chicago and Northwestern (Chicago, Illinois), and Union Pacific (Bethlehem, Pennsylvania) are solid players in the rail segment. American President Companies (Oakland, California) and Sea Containers (Hamilton, Bermuda) are major forces in ocean shipping.

Industrial Testing and Measurement Instruments

Expanded production, the need for greater tolerances, the drive for efficiency and productivity, and an emphasis on world-class quality translates into higher demand for industrial testing and measurement instruments. Companies such as Grandville, Michigan's X-Rite, Inc. (advanced spectrographic testing equipment), and Everett, Washington–based Fluke Corporation (testing and measuring devices) look to ride this tide to higher revenues and profits.

Machine Tools

Both Cincinnati Milicron (Cincinnati, Ohio) and Giddings & Lewis (Fond Du lac, Wisconsin) promise to prosper with a rebound in the international economic environment and an enhanced competitive position against European machine tool companies. According to a study released by Rand's Critical Technologies Institute, "The fortunes of the remaining U.S. machine tool makers are brighter than any point in the last decade."

Telecommunications

Explosive new market opportunities accompany the leapfrog advances in telecommunications technology. Look for industry consolidation and strategic partnerships to tap this huge international market. LDDS WorldCom (Jackson, Mississippi) is a new addition to the big league players in this industry and one to watch.

Specialty Retail

Wal-Mart Stores (Bentonville, Arkansas) led the way and others are following quickly in its profitable path. The Home Depot (Atlanta, Georgia) is the undisputed king in the building supplies arena. Office Depot (Delray Beach, Florida) has captured the largest market share in office products. Pep Boys-Manny, Moe & Jack (Philadelphia, Pennsylvania) keep your car running with auto replacement parts. And now Baby Superstore (Greenville, South Carolina) aims to achieve the same success in the infant clothing market.

Metals

Phelps Dodge will continue to prosper as the economy emerges from the doldrums and demand for copper resumes its upward trend. The Phoenix, Arizona–headquartered company went from near bankruptcy to being the low-cost provider in an internationally competitive mining industry. On the gold front, spinoff Sante Fe Pacific Gold (Albuquerque, New Mexico) looks like a winner with rising gold prices.

Consumer Household/Personal Care Products

Perennial top performer Rubbermaid, Inc. (Wooster, Ohio) keeps its new product mill running (one new product for every day in the year) to generate new demand and higher revenues and earnings. Along those same lines, Towson, Maryland's Black & Decker (power tools) and Fort

Lauderdale, Florida's Sunbeam-Oster (small appliances) power 20 percent earnings per-share growth with innovative products to satisfy consumer needs.

As you search for value in your hometown or local region, you will discover industries and companies with superior growth potential. As you can see from the preceding examples, there are excellent investment opportunities in every part of this nation. You don't have to be on Wall Street to be a successful investor. In fact, you may have an advantage investing from and investing in Main Street, U.S.A.

The Inside Track

Keeping track of the stock holdings of company insiders makes sense but the information must be used with caution. While large and frequent purchases of company stock indicate that management or the board of directors members have considerable faith in the company's future, the meaning of insider sales is less clear. An insider stock sale may not signal poor company prospects but instead result from other circumstances such as personal cash needs to fund college expenses, purchase a new car, or finance a new house.

For information on insider activity, consult *Barron's, Investor's Business Daily, The Wall Street Journal,* Standard & Poor's *The Outlook, Vicker's Weekly Insider Report,* or *The Insiders.*

Insider theory proponents track the insider sales ratio (insider sales divided by insider purchases). If the calculated 10-week moving average is less than 1.5, insiders are selling company shares at a slow pace; this is considered a positive sign. On the other hand, if the ratio rises above 3.0, insiders are heavy sellers, a cautionary sign of overvaluation.

View tracking of insider activity as another tool in your investment toolchest. If it helps you to discover candidates for purchase or sale, use it.

4 Constructing and Positioning Your Portfolio

Portfolio Fundamentals

You don't construct your hometown investment portfolio in a vacuum. You must do so within the framework of an overall investment strategy geared to achieving your investment goals and objectives. In the same vein, your investment strategy must be firmly grounded in fundamental investing principles that have been proven effective over time.

In the pages ahead we will discuss a wide variety of hometown and regional investment opportunities, running the gamut from becoming an angel to providing venture capital and from initial public offerings to municipal bond investments. But to make sure that these investments are appropriate for your portfolio, it is important to take a look at the different types of risk and the methods used to reduce the risk of crippling your overall investment performance.

After all, an investment that is perfect for my investment goals and risk posture may be totally inappropriate for someone else's. Likewise, an investment that performs well in one economic environment may deliver dismal returns or even a loss under different economic conditions. For example, zero coupon bonds earned significant capital gains as interest rates declined steadily until the later part of 1993. However, in today's rising interest rate climate, zero coupon bonds may not be the best place to park your money and preserve your principal from market price fluctuations.

Types of Investment Risk

Interest Rate Risk

As already indicated, changes in interest rates can impact the market value of specific investments. As a general rule, when interest rates decline, the value of existing fixed income investments increases. Conversely, when interest rates rise, the value of existing fixed income investments declines. In the wake of recent Federal Reserve Board interest rate hikes and anticipated future rate increases, it would be foolish to invest a large portion of your portfolio in fixed income securities with long maturities.

The longer the maturity, the greater the degree of interest rate risk. That's why longer-term fixed income investments traditionally pay higher interest rates, to compensate the investor for the higher level of risk.

Business Risk

Changes and cycles in the economic environment also present the investor with risk. Any astute investor takes into account the present and anticipated economic environment when assessing prospective investment opportunities. It would make little sense to purchase local lumber company stocks if the hike in interest rates is expected to cause a major slowdown in the home building industry.

This also carries over into your hometown investing. If your area's economy depends heavily on the health of a major industry and that industry is poised for a contraction with subsequent layoffs, you'll want to think twice before investing in a retail business catering to the employees of your area's large employer. To illustrate, the fortunes of retail businesses in northern Minnesota rely heavily on employees of taconite mining companies to stay in business. The openings and closings of retail businesses on the Iron Range march in lock step with the hirings and layoffs of taconite miners.

Even when you invest in your hometown, you must be aware of what is happening around the rest of the country. Remember, economic activity in other parts of the country can directly impact (both positively and negatively) investment opportunities in your area. Cutbacks in Detroit's automobile industry, a big user of steel produced by taconite ore mined in northern Minnesota, eventually ripples through the raw material chain to cause slowdowns and layoffs in the mining industry, along with tough economic times for hometown businesses and investments.

The business risk associated with certain types of investments such as initial public offerings (IPOs) and private placements is often much higher than that of investing in the stocks and bonds of companies already listed on stock exchanges. Many of these firms are developing new products or technology, entering new markets, and/or starting out on their own after having been shielded from market forces under the corporate umbrella. While the risks are higher, so are the potential rewards. As you will see in Chap. 7, Stephen Globus turned a $100,000 investment into $1 million in three short years.

Market Risk

A variety of factors combine to create market risk, including changing investor and consumer tastes. For example, unless fast food restaurants adjust to demands by consumers for leaner, healthier meals, their business revenues and profits are likely to decline. Other market risk factors are changing technology, labor unrest, management missteps, intensified competition, raw material shortages, natural disasters, and unfavorable regulation. You must weigh the probability of potential market risks occurring and how they will impact your investment.

Once again using northern Minnesota as a case study, labor contract negotiations have typically been less than cordial over the years, at times breaking down into lengthy strikes. Obviously, the start-up of a new business right after the signing of a four-year contract stands a much better chance of avoiding business disruptions due to labor unrest than a business opening its doors on the eve of labor negotiations.

Again, IPOs and private placements represent good examples. Investing in IPOs can entail considerable market risk as "hot" issues go public. High institutional interest and a short supply of stock often result in surging IPO prices on opening day, only to retreat in the weeks and months ahead. The trick is to subscribe to the shares before they open and to purchase IPO shares that are fairly valued based on the company's future prospects and the stock's current price level.

Likewise, private placements face market risk due to their relatively illiquidity. If the company does not intend to go public for at least three years after the private placement, an investor will be hard pressed to leave the deal without taking a loss unless an exit strategy is firmly in place at the outset.

Reinvestment Risk

Reinvestment risk derives from the possibility of having to reinvest your capital at an inopportune time at rates of return substantially lower than current investments.

Laddering your fixed income investments works to help reduce reinvestment risk by having your investments mature over a period of years. By utilizing laddering in a portfolio, investors spread their exposure to reinvestment risk. In a falling interest rate environment, a portion of the portfolio will still be earning the higher interest rates locked in on longer-term securities. In a rising interest scenario, a portion of the portfolio will be maturing to provide the liquidity to take advantage of rising interest rates.

Inflation Risk

The loss of purchasing power represents another investment risk. If inflation outpaces the return earned on a specific investment, you have lost ground. That's why many investors fled certificates of deposit and money market accounts in the early nineties as the rate of inflation outpaced the yield on cash and cash equivalent investments.

Diversification

Investors employ diversification to reduce many types of investment risk. The successful diversification tactics we will discuss are not cast in stone. As the economic environment changes and your investment goals and strategies evolve over time, you will need to fine-tune how you diversify to reduce your risk posture. More likely than not, the successful investor will need to utilize a number of the following diversification techniques.

At the basis of all diversification strategies is the goal of avoiding the risks associated with having "all your eggs in one basket" and then having that basket turned upside down by changing economic forces. While investing in initial public offerings (IPOs) may be a smart investment strategy for a portion of your investment portfolio, no sane investor would suggest putting 100 percent of your portfolio in IPOs or that all market conditions were conducive to successful IPO investing.

Company Diversification

The most obvious method of adding breadth to your investment portfolio lies in avoiding risking all your available financial resources on one company.

One of the proposed diversification strategies, the Rule of Eight, contends that a minimum of eight stocks is required to properly achieve enough protection to prevent the occurrence of an unpredictable event to any single stock from devastating the overall value of your investment portfolio.

Limiting the amount of money, by aggregate or percentage, invested in any one stock or investment ranks as a top investment strategy and wealth preserver.

Industry Diversification

Just as individual companies and their stocks can run into trouble and fall out of favor with investors, whole industries can encounter turbulent times when company and industry revenues and earnings decline drastically and company stock prices suffer steep declines.

Industry fallout occurs for a host of reasons. Cyclical industries such as automobile, metals, timber, and steel undergo periodic economic cycles as the economy expands and contracts. Investing heavily in a single industry needlessly exposes your portfolio to significant risks and investment losses should the industry sector or the economy in general suffer reverses.

Not only is it wise to diversify your investment by industry. It also makes good sense to keep a close pulse on industry health and the economic, political, and other factors that can wreak havoc with revenues and earnings. Investing a portion of your portfolio in hometown and area companies and other investments allows you to observe these forces firsthand.

Geographical Diversification

Just as you would steer away from investing in any one company or industry, you need to avoid investing all your capital in one geographic area. In the late 1980s and early 1990s, investors with their total portfolio invested in California (companies, real estate, banks, etc.) heightened their risk of losses as the California economy went through one aftershock after another (riots, contraction of the silicon valley computer industry, foreign competition, earthquakes, fires, and restrictive business legislation).

Today, with the proliferation of American depositary receipts (ADRs), as well as foreign country, global, and international mutual funds, geographic diversification takes on a brand new dimension.

Asset Allocation

Positioning yourself in the right asset categories can improve your investment performance. Too few individuals construct their portfolios within the framework of a sensible, preestablished investment policy or strategy. Most portfolios tend to be product-driven (individual stock, bonds or other investments) rather than strategy-driven, resulting in portfolios that are both inappropriately structured to achieve the desired investment objectives and unprofitable.

Take the time to define your investment goals and follow through with well researched and thought-out asset allocation investment selection that's consistent with your goals. Simply stated, asset allocation seeks to minimize investment risk with a spreading of portfolio assets among different investment alternatives.

Assessing Your Risk Posture

Investors must assess their risk tolerance levels in determining an investment strategy. A well crafted diversification strategy can greatly reduce your exposure to investment risk.

You need to thoroughly examine your risk posture before you undertake defining and implementing your investment strategy. It's a critical element in successful investing.

Within the framework of specific risk tolerances, you can construct your investment strategy and portfolio. It's also important to remember that your risk tolerance changes as your financial circumstances, age, family obligations, and anticipated capital requirements vary over time.

A young person has more time to recoup from investment setbacks and can take on a more aggressive stance in developing a portfolio mix. On the other hand, a retired person requiring an income stream from current investments to meet ongoing living expenses probably needs to establish a more conservative investment posture.

Life Cycle Investing

Life cycle investing takes into account life stages and adjusts portfolios to achieve a desired performance level within specific risk parameters to meet anticipated financial obligations.

According to life cycle investing theory, individuals move through different life cycles with a different set of investment goals and risk tolerances associated with each stage of the life cycle.

Typically, younger investors adopt a higher risk posture to earn higher returns and build up their wealth. If they incur losses during this earlier stage of their life, they have time to recoup with subsequent investments.

On the other hand, older investors tend to gravitate toward the lower end of the risk/return relationship, desiring to preserve existing wealth and its income flow.

Hometown Investment Tactics

Short Selling

Just as you have to adjust your portfolio mix in reaction to changing economic conditions, you also need to adjust your investment tactics when circumstances present themselves. Too many investors sit idly waiting for down markets to pass by, thereby missing excellent investment opportunities. Unfortunately, many investors fail to realize that just as much money, if not substantially more, can be made on the downside of a market move as on its upside.

When stock prices start heading south, it's time to seriously consider selling short, in effect selling stocks you don't own. Remember that every successful coach depends on his or her defensive unit to play an integral role in the overall winning strategy. The same holds true for a successful investment strategy.

Being a hometown investor can give you a significant edge over long investors and other short sellers. News of slowdowns and layoffs often hits main street long before they happen, giving you the jump on other investors. You can position your investment before the news hits the national press and starts to negatively impact the firm's stock price.

Despite belief to the contrary, the basic short selling strategy is simple. You sell a borrowed stock now at a high price with the anticipation of purchasing it back at a lower price later for a profit. Short selling rests on your conviction, after proper analysis, that stock prices in general or for a specific company will drop in the weeks and months ahead.

The financial facts of life dictate that you must keep your investment capital at work during all times of the investment cycle to maximize your return. Get your defense on the field during down markets and take advantage of management fumbles with well thought-out and executed short selling.

During bull markets and hot IPO markets, euphoria takes over and stock prices tend to get bid up over their underlying values. Even in the midst of the recent prolonged recession or economic stagnation, stock market prices continued to hit new highs, seemingly defying reality.

It would appear that only a complete fool would be selling stocks in the face of a continuing bull market. But don't kid yourself. There have been ample opportunities for short selling profits during the recent market rise in light of volatile price swings in the market overall, in market segments, and in particular stocks.

The explosion in state-sanctioned gaming operations created a frenzy that sent the stock prices of gaming industry companies soaring. Market rationale went out the window when newly issued gaming stocks—with no prior track record, shaky financials, and poor earnings prospects or even losses—shot up to new highs week after week.

To be sure, quality gaming firms such as International Gaming Technology with secure market share, strong domestic and overseas franchises, and proven technology should continue to hit paydirt in the revenues and earnings columns. However, the spurt in gaming firm stock prices clearly represented the impressive fundamentals of the quality firms pulling along the mediocre firms. In other words, a dramatic shakeout in the gaming industry firms and their stock prices was the perfect scenario for uncovering short selling candidates.

Investors who identified all the classic overvaluation signs profited handsomely from short selling gaming stocks as they tumbled from record highs to a fraction of their former prices during 1994.

To participate in the world of short selling, it is important to know and understand the game rules. First of all, to sell short you have to establish a margin account with your broker. You will need to put up either cash or marginable securities as collateral.

With the current 50 percent margin rules in effect, you can short $2 worth of stock for every $1 worth of collateral residing in your margin account. It's wise to keep a collateral safety cushion to prevent unwanted margin calls from forcing you out of a stock or short position.

Don't look for dividends to help increase your short position investment return. Any dividends accruing to the stock belong to the owner of the stock, the person from whom the shorted stock was borrowed.

A short sale must always be made at either a price higher than the last sale or at the same price of the last sale, if the last preceeding change in the security's price was upward. In no case can a short sale take place at a price lower than the previous sale. This is called the *short sale, uptick,* or *plus tick* rule.

The purpose of the uptick rule is to prevent short selling action from driving the price of a particular security down further in a declining market and potentially causing a panic situation and downward price spiral. This rule can also result in your broker's taking longer to complete your short trade.

Short Do's and Don'ts

Keep your finger on the pulse of the companies you plan on shorting. Know how anticipated changes in the economic, political, legal, and social environments can impact their future performance and the level of their stock prices.

Stock market trends represent an important barometer for the short seller. The old stock market adage, "The trend is your friend," goes double for this strategy.

Stay away from stocks continuing to make new highs. Don't let the expectation that they must tumble soon cloud your investment analysis. Momentum is a powerful stock market force and must be reckoned with. Wait for a consolidation and pullback for indications of a slowdown, then look for confirmation of a sustainable price reversal.

Closely related to the high price scenario, the high price/earnings (P/E) ratio method of ferreting out companies whose stocks should be sold short often fails to produce profitable results. Again, it's hard to fight momentum. P/E ratios may help locate potential stocks that could be sold short in the future, but you need more evidence before you place the stock on the final short selling list.

Don't let economic forces or high stock prices keep you from increasing your investment gains. Use short selling as a useful tool to profit from overvalued situations.

Rocky Mountain Short Selling Candidate

In my neck of the woods, I can readily think of a short selling candidate that would have made savvy investors a good bit of change over the past several years. As a resident of the Rocky Mountain area and a subscriber to U.S. West telephone service, I did not have to be a supersleuth to see that U.S. West had its share of problems.

More often than not, when you picked up *The Denver Post, Rocky Mountain News, Casper Star-Tribune,* or other regional newspaper, you could find an article about communities and states complaining about the poor quality of service provided by U.S. West. Not a very conducive environment for proposed rate increases.

In late 1993, the company made front page news in *Investor's Business Daily* and other business publications when it announced plans to eliminate some 9000 jobs and take a $3.8 billion charge against third quarter earnings. U.S. West had already incurred a loss of $614 million or $1.49 per share in 1992 and would likely post a loss in excess of $2.8 billion or $6.60 per share in 1993.

Actually, it was old news to me. My telephone repair man had long before mentioned that U.S. West's Cheyenne operations would be consolidated with the loss of many jobs (that took place in 1994). It isn't hard to put two and two together and determine that Cheyenne cutbacks weren't the only ones on the chopping block.

A short sale of U.S. West stock in October 1993 could have taken place around the $48 per share level. Since then U.S. West's stock price has trended steadily downward, hitting a low around $35 per share in 1994.

Obviously, you would not go out and short a stock based on one conversation with your telephone repair man. But it's a great place to begin your investigative work, and it gives you the jump on the market that can turn a modest investment gain into a substantial gain by establishing your position before the market move.

What are U.S. West's prospects for the future and where is its stock price headed? I'll let you know the next time lightning strikes and my telephone repair man comes to call.

Shortex, an investment newsletter specializing in recommending short sales, is published by Technomart R.G.A., Inc. A yearly subscription sells for $279 while a six-month trial offer for 10 issues runs $159. To order, contact Technomart at 6669 Security Boulevard, Suite 103, Baltimore, Maryland 21207-4014, or call 800-877-6555 for information.

You can use short sale recommendations on firms outside your area to highlight industries within your region that may also be in trouble. On the other hand, the troubles of one firm may represent market opportunities for local companies that compete with troubled companies recommended for short selling.

For example, the January 26, 1995 issue of *Shortex* listed Dallas, Texas-based Oryx Energy Company as a short candidate due to shrinking assets and depleting reserves to pay off debt. *Shortex* highlighted little resistance to the selloff, which drove Oryx's stock price below its 200-day moving average.

As a Dallas, Texas hometown investor, you could analyze whether this situation was isolated to Oryx or was an industrywide condition sure to negatively impact other oil and gas exploration firms in your region. Either way, you could make out. If the trend was industrywide, short selling other oil and gas exploration firms might be in order. Conversely, better positioned competitors—such as Schlumberger Limited, a New York–headquartered company but with plenty of interests in Texas—might be able to capitalize on Oryx's misfortune by picking up exploration assets and reserves at dirt cheap prices as Oryx scrambles for cash.

By keeping up on your business press readings, you would have noticed Jack Egan's February 20, 1995 "On Money" column in *U.S. News &*

World Report that discussed a potential spurt in energy services stocks. Likewise, your comp subscription to the American Gas Association would have provided you with a copy of "The Natural Gas Industry: A Sound Investment for Today and Tomorrow," which gave a detailed review of the industry and its long-term prospects.

Turnaround Situations

Tracking the corporate turnaround can return big investment gains for the patient investor. While investing in turnaround situations clearly comes complete with unique risks (including bankruptcy), the savvy investor can temper those risks with careful investigative work.

Taking a contrarian approach and searching for underlying value in turnaround situations can help you beat both the odds and the market. A company does not have to be courting bankruptcy to qualify as a moneymaking turnaround situation for the investor who is willing to do some up-front work and take on a measured degree of risk.

A turnaround represents a positive change in the fortunes of a company that can stem from many different factors, both internal and external to the firm. The turnaround represents a special situation where the individual hometown investor has an edge on and can outperform Wall Street's professional money managers.

A number of factors can contribute to the company having difficult times and falling out of favor with Wall Street. Ineffective top management can be squandering market opportunities and market share with inappropriate product, marketing, and operation strategies. Undercapitalization, excessive debt, and poor financial planning can lead to cash flow crises and lost expansion opportunities. Technological innovation can leave the company at a competitive disadvantage with outmoded production facilities and/or outdated product lines.

Outside factors can also negatively impact the firm's ability to compete and result in declining revenues and profits. Of course, general economic and industry conditions impact a firm's financial results. Scarce raw material price hikes or the sudden unavailability of key raw materials can spell doom for companies without adequate contingency material sources.

Other reasons for a company's economic misfortunes include:

- Loss of a major customer due to competition, bankruptcy, or other reason.
- Governmental regulation such as newly enacted stringent environmental requirements.

- Natural disasters such as earthquakes or fires that disrupt production operations.
- Shifting customer preferences.
- Labor problems.
- Intense foreign competition.

It's important to remember that not all distressed companies represent turnaround situations. Some company's operating results and stock prices have been driven down for good reason and without a realistic chance of recovery. You must learn to separate the promising ones from the true dogs.

Turnaround situations furnish the opportunity for you to profit from new and unusual developments from within both the firm and its surrounding environment. Unlike most other investment situations, the individual investor can learn about them and invest in these special situations before the general market and institutions bid up the stock prices. As a hometown investor, you'll be in tune with positive actions taken by local management and be aware of renewed activity at the company's facilities.

Turnarounds routinely take many months and years to accomplish. There's plenty of time to do your sleuthing and make inquiries with plant managers about how things are going down at XYZ Corporation.

Reports of declining earnings and falling stock prices, lackluster near-term prospects, negative publicity and uncertainties clouding the future of troubled companies drive away most potential investors, pushing the stock price down further. Once you see actions being taken to effectively deal with the problems and encouraging signs that the strategies are starting to work, it's time to stake your claim before the turnaround in progress garners national attention. Here's where you put your local and regional press coverage to good use.

On the institutional front, many mutual funds and other institutional investors abide by investment guidelines, which prohibit their investing in companies that don't pay dividends or that fail to meet other specific criteria. This places downward pressure on the stock prices of potential turnaround candidates, increasing the disparity between market valuation and intrinsic value.

Likewise, as the turnaround company's fortunes improve and institutions can once again take a position in the stock, increasing institutional demand translates into upward price pressure. All of this works to the benefit of the turnaround investor who initiated his or her position after selling pressure drove the stock down and before newfound demand started driving the stock price back up again.

A management change signals one of the sure signs of a turnaround attempt in process. These moves will hit the local rumor mills and regional news well before they are picked up by the national financial press, once again giving you important lead time to outmaneuver and outperform the professional money managers. Publications such as *Crain's Cleveland Business* and *Colorado Business* regularly list management changes and promotions. These are often early signals in the changing fortunes of a troubled company.

You'll be in the information pipeline for news about restructuring announcements, shedding of divisions or subsidiaries, plant consolidations, mass employee layoffs, and large writeoffs—all early warning signs of an attempted turnaround in progress.

While new management may not be the all-clear signal to jump right in, it is a great indicator that you should begin seriously evaluating a company's turnaround prospects. By keeping a pulse on the new management's strategies and actions, you will be able to tell how the turnaround attempt is progressing.

Your overall evaluation should consider three critical factors.

- First of all, assess the financial viability of the troubled company. Don't waste time and energy on companies with poor prospects of turning around. This involves looking at its debt level and debt servicing requirements.
- Second, determine whether the company can make a strong earnings rebound. This requires analyzing the reasons for the firm's misfortunes. Is an economic contraction, industry cycle, or a product life cycle at the root of the problem? How will anticipated changes in those scenarios impact the company and its ability to bounce back?
- Third, evaluate management and its restructuring strategies. Is management undertaking the correct actions to improve the situation? Are there key acquisitions in the works? What new and innovative marketing avenues are they trying? Look at the changes to determine whether the turnaround seems plausible.

A host of questions need to be answered. Evaluate each of the company's crucial operations from manufacturing to marketing and from finances to research and development to get a feel for how the company is handling problem areas. Equally important, get a feel for factors external to the company that can impact, either positively or negatively, the firm's operational and financial standing.

Most of this material you can glean from the company's financial reports. But put it to the litmus test of comparing what the management is saying and what it is doing by what you actually see happening at the company's plants, retail outlets, and/or other operations in your area.

Spinoff Companies

Dick Irvin of Columbia Falls, Montana used his knowledge of his area's timber industry gained from years of operating a Montana-based trucking company to parlay a broker's recommendation on an upcoming Burlington Resources, Inc. spinoff (itself an earlier successful spinoff from Burlington Northern, Inc.) into a nice profit. Irvin purchased units of Plum Creek Timber Company, L.P. in June 1989 at $6⅜ per share (adjusted for 3-for-1 stock split in December 1993). He more than quintupled his original investment by 1994, before the stock retreated. In addition, the partnership units yielded around 7 percent with steadily increasing dividends (five dividend increases since the company went public in 1989). (For an updated investment analysis of Plum Creek Timber Company, L.P. refer to Chap. 7.)

Companies have been spinning off divisions, subsidiaries, and other corporate units for decades. Some spinoffs are true losers that are being shed solely for the purpose of eliminating the drag they inflict on overall corporate financial results. Others reflect opportunities for investors to capitalize on the unrecognized value of the spun-off assets or the unrealized potential of the spun-off business once it has been unshackled by a less than enthusiastic or supportive corporate management.

Without a doubt, not all spinoff companies turn out to be success stories. But the world of corporate spinoffs is a fertile field, offering ample opportunities for huge capital gains for the investor willing to do some individual investigative work.

While most research analysts and major market players ignore the spinoff company due to a lack of information and understanding of the firm's business, individual investors can take advantage of this type of undervalued special situation for exactly the same reason. Again, hometown investors, who are familiar with local or area operations that are being spun off, have a distinct advantage over Wall Street money managers who are far from the action.

To first determine how spinoffs get undervalued in the first place, look at some of the misconceptions and realities about these corporate orphans and the real reasons companies dispose of them.

Too often, it's assumed that the only reason a parent company sheds an operation is because it is a "dog" with little chance of improving earnings or because the new firm operates in a lackluster industry with little chance for growth. However, some operations or divisions are casting off to shareholders or the public for reasons that do not reflect poorly on the new firm or its ability to succeed or even flourish under its newly found independence.

For example, when Burlington Resources decided to spin off its Plum Creek Timber operations, it was not because they weren't profitable or well run. Instead, the timber lands and resources did not fit in with the Burlington Resources' management's decision to focus that company's financial and personnel resources on its oil and gas exploration activities.

A number of other major factors impact the decision to spin off a company operation. Analysts tend to specialize in market niches or industries and have trouble valuing nonmainline assets. As a result, diversified companies fall victim to valuations that as a whole would be less than the separate valuations of the sum of the corporate parts. Thus, the spinoff is one way management can unleash the value of those operations to shareholders by releasing them from the shadow of the corporate umbrella. Since most oil and gas analysts would have a hard time fairly valuing timber resources, more likely than not Burlington Resources as a company was undervalued in the market.

Evidence of that undervaluation is borne out by the initial offering price of $6⅜ per share (adjusted for December 1993 3-for-1 stock split for Plum Creek Timber Company master partnership interest units). By the end of 1992, Plum Creek's stock price jumped to $15 per share and peaked at $32½ per share in 1994.

After the spinoff, there may be downside price pressure due to institutional selling. Institutional investors may sell their shares for several reasons. The new company's shares may not meet the investment policy of the bank trust department, insurance company, mutual fund, pension fund, or other institutional investor in regard to industry exposure, liquidity, or credit constraints. In reality, the investment manager may not have any choice but to sell the newly acquired shares without regard to investment potential, if only to resolve violation of its investment guidelines.

This creates buying opportunities for the attentive investor. As time goes on, the organizational changes usually associated with the new firms start to induce superior operating performance. The improved operating results get recognized by the market, resulting in higher demand for their shares and higher share prices. Finally, a number of spinoffs attract takeover bids from suitors who recognize their undervalued situation. All these can lead to significant investment gains.

How do you get started in this unique investment niche? First you must be aware of upcoming spinoffs. *The Wall Street Journal* routinely covers most, if not all, proposed disposals in its daily dividend announcement section. Likewise, *Investor's Business Daily* and other financial publications regularly report on proposed spinoffs. This will keep you on a par with other investors around the country, but keeping appraised of potential changes within companies in your own hometown or region can alert you to potential opportunities well ahead of the financial press. Remember, time is money when you can establish your position ahead of other investors.

Once you're hot on the trail, one of the best sources of information on the new companies is the parent firm of the proposed spinoff. Contact the firm's Financial or Legal Department and request a copy of the SEC-required Information Statement, SEC Form 10, which includes a five-year history of the newly created company. Then find a comfortable chair and get prepared to wade through some 100-plus pages of data, a great deal of it stultifying, boring, legal verbiage. Also request past copies of the parent company's annual reports, and SEC Form 10Ks for the past three years as well as releases pertaining to the spinoff.

All this information will provide you with a solid foundation for your analysis. It includes data on the proposed company's main lines of business, business history, business properties, affiliated companies, competition, depth of management experience, amount of director and executive participation in company ownership, debt structure, liquidity and capital resources, factors impacting operating results and company outlook.

Look for competitive advantages that can give the spinoff company an edge over industry competitors.

- Does it possess patents or trademarks?
- Does its market niche allow it to command higher-than-normal prices and margins?
- Do high entry costs prevent additional competition from entering the industry in the future?
- Does it have the financial wherewithal to capitalize on the industry's consolidation, either through strategic acquisitions or aggressive marketing actions to capture additional market share?
- Are capital expenditures keeping the company's equipment and production processes at state-of-the-art levels?
- Are research and development expenses geared to the development of new products?
- Does the firm's future depend on a few major customers or on government contracts susceptible to the budget cutting process?
- How do current backlogs compare with previous years' backlogs? Is the trend upward or downward?

- Does the company have alternative raw material sources to alleviate interruptions in raw material supplies or significant rises in raw material prices?
- How will cyclical economic forces impact future operations and profitability?
- What has been the firm's history of labor relations?
- Is the company unionized?
- What is the recent strike history?
- Will the company be able to implement cost-cutting strategies without incurring extended and costly work interruptions?
- Does management possess the industry knowledge and expertise to make the right decisions?
- Is this the same management that produced the lackluster performance in past years, or has there been an infusion of new blood and corporate restructuring to improve operations?

Take a good, hard look at the financial statements.

- Have revenues and margins held steady, or are competition and higher costs taking their toll on profitability?
- Will the firm generate adequate cash flow to fund needed capital expenditures, research and development, and market expansion?
- Is the company debt-heavy?
- Will debt servicing cause a cash crunch if planned revenues fail to materialize?
- How secure are the company's lines of credit?
- When do they expire, and how do their rates compare with the current interest environment? After all, the rates lenders charge reflect the degree of confidence they have in the company's ability to repay the amounts borrowed.

Review the reasons behind extraordinary charges or credits to company financial results.

- Are they likely to happen again in the future?
- Do they promise to improve or hinder future financial performance?
- How successful has the company assimilated past acquisitions?

- Have they gone smoothly, or has the company had to charge writeoffs for past acquisitions gone awry?

Evaluate how external forces can impact the spinoff company's operations.

- Will the firm take on significant legal liabilities as the result of its newfound independence?
- Can environmental actions or a change in government regulations impact the firm's cost structure or its ability to remain a competitive force in the industry?

It's also a good idea to get a handle on the competition and industry trends. Request copies of the annual reports and Form 10-Ks from major competitors.

- How does their financial performance—in terms of revenues, costs of goods sold, administrative and selling overhead, margins, and net income—compare with that of the spinoff company?
- What differences are there in capital structure and debt load? How will they affect the company's competitive position?

Read both management's discussions of operating results and their perspectives of major trends in their industry carefully. Are they similar or at opposite ends of the spectrum?

After your analysis convinces you that the company's prospects are good and that the stock price is either undervalued or fairly valued, it's time to put your money to work earning substantial profits.

Be on the alert for potential spinoffs in the works. Keeping in close communication with his regional broker put Dick Irwin onto the path of Plum Creek Timber Company, L.P. and a solid investment gain. The same hometown investment strategy can work for you.

PART 2

Hometown Investment Options

In Part 1, we looked at how the hometown investor can put local, regional, and national resources to work in evaluating potential hometown investments for superior investment gains. Starting with Chap. 5, we will investigate and analyze the different types of investments that hometown investors can use to construct their portfolios. Put the resources and contacts discussed in the first four chapters to use in the remainder of the book as they are appropriate to your circumstances.

5
Taking a Municipal Approach

One of the easiest ways to take advantage of backyard investments is purchasing municipal bonds. What could be closer to hometown investing than buying municipal securities that fund local and regional infrastructure projects such as roads, sewers and water treatment plants, schools, municipal buildings, and economic development projects? Municipal bonds can also be issued by states, state authorities, and local governments to cover that government's general financing requirements.

The municipal bond market represents a $1.2 trillion securities market with more than 50,000 state, municipal, and other government bodies issuing municipal bonds. There's plenty of alternative municipal investments to meet the needs of any portfolio.

In the aftermath of the Tax Reform Act of 1986, municipal bonds emerged as one of few remaining investments with tax-favored status, thus making them very popular with investors subject to high tax rates.

"Municipals are one of the last great tax shelters. A 6½ percent AAA long municipal bond equates to a 11½ percent taxable equivalent yield for people who live in places like Virginia and The District of Columbia with tax rates in the 46 percent range," says Herbert Davidson, Senior Vice President with Meyers, Pollock, Robbins, Inc. based in McLean, Virginia.

The benefits of municipal bonds are even more dramatic in the state of New York where the tax rate equals 53 percent. A New York resident would have to earn a taxable return of 13¼ percent to match the return on tax sheltered 6½ percent municipal bonds.

Interest earned on municipal securities is exempt from federal income taxes (with the exception of the alternative minimum tax calculation) and in some cases also exempt from state and local income tax. Obviously, their tax-exempt status makes municipals more acceptable for nontax-sheltered investment accounts. Since IRAs (individual retirement accounts) already possess tax shelter status, it doesn't make good economic sense to purchase municipal securities for IRAs or for other tax-sheltered retirement accounts.

To be sure, you must compare the yield on a tax-exempt municipal security with that offered by a taxable investment of similar quality to see which makes more sense in your financial and tax situation. Table 5-1 provides a comparison of tax-exempt and taxable yields for different income levels.

To determine the taxable equivalent yield, divide the tax-free yield by 1 minus the tax rate, as follows:

$$\text{Taxable equivalent yield} = \text{Tax-free yield}/(1 - \text{Tax rate})$$

Assuming a 6 percent tax-free yield and a tax rate of 31 percent, the taxable equivalent yield comes out to 8.70 percent.

$$\text{Taxable equivalent yield} = 6.0/(1 - 31\% \text{ Tax rate})$$
$$= 8.70\%$$

Despite the fact that in 1995 interest rates were inching higher as the Federal Reserve Bank attempted to cool down the economy, the future looks promising for municipal bonds investors. In addition to substantial tax benefits, there are other solid reasons for taking a serious look at municipals. First of all, the dramatic slowdown in supply of new municipal bond investments means that demand will push up prices of existing municipal bonds as smart investors seek to reduce the tax bite and enhance their after-tax return.

Table 5-1. Tax-Exempt/Taxable Yield Equivalents

	Tax-free yield (%)				
Income tax bracket (%)	4.00	5.00	5.5	6.00	6.5
		*Equivalent taxable yields**			
15	4.70	5.80	6.47	7.06	7.65
28	5.55	6.94	7.64	8.33	9.03
31	5.79	7.24	7.97	8.70	9.42
36	6.25	7.81	8.59	9.38	10.16
39.6	6.62	8.27	9.10	9.93	10.76

*Does not take into account the impact of state and local income taxes, which would increase the equivalent yield.

"For the serious long-term municipal investor there are both an attractive yield and long-term capital appreciation opportunities," says Davidson.

Second, the trend in government (both state and federal) has been to impose higher tax rates, not lower. Therefore, the tax-sheltered aspects of municipals will become even more attractive in the coming years of raised tax levels.

Third, the Securities and Exchange Commission approved new rules in November 1994 increasing the disclosure on municipal bonds, providing investors with new information to more accurately price municipal bonds and learn about important events that could impact municipal bond market prices. These new rules were being phased in through January 1996.

Fourth, the Public Securities Association, an industry trade group, is also planning a 900-telephone number that will provide investors with on-the-spot municipal pricing and other trade information. This will help municipal bond investors make more informed investment decisions.

Revenue and General Obligation Bonds

The two major categories of municipal securities consist of revenue bonds and general obligation bonds. Typically, *revenue* (or *project*) *bonds* are issued to finance a project, such as a water treatment plant or highway, that is projected to earn enough income from fees to repay the principal plus interest on the bonds. On the other hand, *general obligation bonds* are backed by the taxing authority of the issuer. For this reason, general obligation bonds are usually considered more secure investments than revenue bonds since projected user fee revenues from revenue bond projects might fall short of expectations.

When considering investing in municipal bonds, it's crucial to evaluate the credit quality of the issuing body and how repayment of the debt plus interest will be accomplished. Since your maturity value is established in advance, the only risk to your principal (if you don't sell your municipal bonds before maturity) lies in the potential for default by the issuing body. This possibility was painfully brought to the attention of investors in Orange County, California municipal bonds.

As noted, the strongest municipal guarantee comes in the form of a general obligation security backed by the taxing power of the state or of the jurisdiction issuing the municipal security. Funds to repay the debt derive from specified taxes or fees collected, such as highway tolls or special sales tax levies. On the other hand, the accreted interest on revenue bonds is paid out of revenues financed by the capital borrowed. Since these bonds must generate adequate cash flow before investors can be repaid, they are considered less financially secure investments than those backed by the taxing authority of the issuing jurisdiction.

Independent rating agencies assess the ability of municipal bond issuers to repay their debt, assigning ratings indicating the relative safety against default of each specific issue. Fitch Investor's Service, Inc., Moody's Investor Service, and Standard & Poor's Corporation review and analyze the jurisdiction's financial standing and debt coverage capabilities for a particular issue to give it an investment grade.

Table 5-2 illustrates the bond rating classifications from the Fitch Investor's Service, Inc.'s *Rating Register.* This highlights the degree of risk associated with each rating classification. It's important to know and understand how a particular municipal bond rating fits into your personal investment risk posture before you invest.

The rating registers of Fitch and other rating services also provide additional information such as:

- Conditional ratings premised on the successful completion of a project or occurrence of a specific event.
- Ratings suspension when the amount of information available from the issuer is deemed not adequate for rating purposes.
- Withdrawn ratings when the issuer fails to provide proper and timely information or when an issue is called or refinanced.
- "Alerts" designed to notify investors of the occurrence of an event that is likely to result in a rating change and the likely direction of such change.

Ratings below BBB carry higher degrees of speculative risk in terms of payment of interest and repayment of principal. For example, bonds rated BB are considered speculative with the obligor's ability to pay interest and repay principal possibly affected over time by adverse economic conditions. However, business and financial alternatives can be identified that could assist the obligor in satisfying its debt service requirements.

Ratings changes are listed, showing the previous and current rating and the effective date of rating change. Each rating service maintains its own credit assessment procedures and ratings. The basic thrust behind each rating, however, remains the same: to provide investors with an informed judgment on the credit quality of a municipal bond. Ratings registers or manuals can be found at most city or university libraries.

Issues with the maximum assurance against default rate the highest, or AAA, rating. For example, top-quality issues earn an AAA rating as do

Table 5-2. Investment-Grade Bond Ratings

Symbol	*Description*
AAA	Bonds considered to be investment grade and of the highest credit quality. The obligor has an exceptionally strong ability to pay interest and repay principal, which is unlikely to be affected by reasonably foreseeable events. Maximum safety.
AA	Bonds considered to be investment grade and of very high credit quality. The obligor's ability to pay interest and repay principal is very strong, although not quite as strong as bonds rated AAA. Because bonds rated in the AAA and AA categories are not significantly vulnerable to foreseeable future developments, short-term debt of these issuers is generally rated F-1+. Very high grade.
A	Bonds considered to be investment grade and of high credit quality. The obligor's ability to pay interest and repay principal is considered to be strong, but may be more vulnerable to adverse changes in economic conditions and circumstances than bonds with higher ratings. High grade.
BBB	Bonds considered to be investment grade and of satisfactory credit quality. The obligor's ability to pay interest and repay principal is considered to be adequate. Adverse changes in economic conditions and circumstances, however, are more likely to have adverse impact on these bonds and therefore impair timely payment. Good grade.
Plus (+)/ Minus (–)	Plus and minus signs are used with a rating symbol to indicate the relative position of a credit within the rating category. Plus and minus signs, however, are not used in the AAA category.
Trend and Indicator	Trend indicators show whether credit fundamentals are improving, stable, declining, or uncertain as follows: Improving ↑ Stable ↔ Declining ↓ Uncertain ↕ It is important to note that trend indicators are not predictions that any rating change will, in fact, occur.
R	Indicates that Fitch does not rate a specific issue.

"escrowed" municipal bonds, those in which the issuer has purchased U.S. government bonds or deposited compensating balances in a depositary bank to act as collateral for the municipal bond debt.

Insured municipal bonds, with a financial guarantee of additional backing to ensure repayment of principal and interest, can also achieve an AAA rating. For example, the Municipal Bond Investors Assurance Corporation (MBIA) and others have backed in excess of 30 percent of municipal bonds issued in recent years. The insurance backing, with its AAA rating status, gives municipal bond investors added credit assurance since the insuring company has conducted an independent comprehensive credit review before backing a specific bond issue. The insuring company guarantees that scheduled interest payments and principal due at maturity will be made without interruption, thus protecting the investor from default on the bond. Investors with insured Orange County municipal bonds will fare much better than their uninsured counterparts.

Lower ratings, such as AA and A, still represent quality issues but with less protection against possible default. As indicated, municipal bonds rated BBB represent the lowest of investment grade securities.

You have to weigh your own investment goals and the risk posture you are comfortable assuming, but generally conservative investors should stick with A or above ratings on municipal zeros and AA for long-term investments. As with other types of investments, higher-quality issues typically carry lower interest rates and vice versa.

Zero Coupon Municipal Bonds

Municipal zero coupon bonds are issued by state and local government jurisdictions to raise money for public purposes, but they often come with call features. This means the issuer can redeem the zero before maturity after a certain date and under certain conditions. Clearly, a call feature can have an impact on the actual overall yield.

To illustrate, assume you purchase a municipal zero coupon with an interest rate of 8 percent. If interest rates decline substantially after the issue date, it would make sense for the issuing jurisdiction to call or retire the bonds, in compliance with the terms of the call provision, to eliminate the high-cost debt and replace it with other debt paying lower interest rates. If the zero coupon bonds are called, your investment, which had been earning 8 percent, will have to be reinvested, most likely at significantly lower yields.

Make sure you know the call provisions and how they can affect your anticipated yield. Municipal coupon bonds paying the same stated interest rate and maturing at the same time could possess radically different call provisions. It pays to check out the fine print.

For example, one municipal zero coupon bond could be callable after two years of issue by paying 102 percent of compound accreted value, while another otherwise similar municipal might not be callable until after five years of issue and paying 105 percent of compound accreted value. The second bond thus provides substantially longer interest rate protection and a much higher retirement payoff.

Usually, municipal zeros are not callable until five or ten years after issue; so the time remaining to the call date becomes the critical issue. This time period to call date is termed *call protection.*

Even if your issue is recalled, it may not affect you. Some recalls may be not for the entire issue but only for zeros of a certain serial number. Don't depend on the luck of the draw. Try to obtain yield to call that remains competitive with yield to maturity so that your investment return will not be significantly hurt by a municipal zero coupon bond recall.

To choose the proper investment for you, your decision-making process should include consideration of:

- The stated interest rate.
- Call provisions.
- Maturity date.
- Yield to maturity.
- Yield to call date.
- Issue investment grade rating.
- Your investment goals.
- Risk tolerance.

The popularity of municipal zero coupon bonds among investors is evidenced in the amount issued each year. For each of the three years 1990 through 1992, more than $4 billion in zero coupon municipals hit the streets and were gobbled up by investors large and small.

Government talk of raising marginal personal income tax rates and eliminating even more tax shelters promises to make the tax-exempt municipal zero coupon bond even more enticing to middle- and upper-income investors in the future.

Innovations in the zero coupon bond field in recent years include the *convertible zero coupon municipal bond.* These bonds start their lives as zero coupon bonds, and, after a stated period of generally 8 to 15 years, they convert to interest-paying bonds. The main attraction is for investors nearing retirement. They can earn tax-sheltered interest until retirement, then receive the interest stream in cash to enhance their retirement cash flow to meet living expenses.

Another variation of the municipal zero coupon bond comes in the form of *stripped municipals.* In this case, these municipals pay interest semiannually on coupons that are stripped from the bond. The bond still sells at a deep discount from face value.

Locking in Attractive Rates

In late 1994, high-grade municipal bonds yielded around 6.5 percent. Comparing that to an inflation rate of approximately 2.7 percent, investors could lock in a "real return" approaching 4 percent, much higher than the historic norm and sheltered from the tax bite. Shop around to get the best price available.

Another factor is entering into the attractiveness of municipal bonds. Through the first seven months of 1994, new municipal bond supply decreased 40 percent compared with the same period in 1993. The slowdown in the supply of municipal bonds has worked to create additional investor interest in municipal issues trading in the secondary market, thus pushing up prices.

The shortage of municipals has created market voids where investors are having difficulty locating the right security in terms of the right coupon, credit, and maturity for their investment purposes. The supply is especially tight in such states as California, Florida, Michigan, New York, Pennsylvania, and Texas where new municipal issues have dwindled.

The market shortage could continue to drive up prices unless more new issues come to market. This scenario is likely to continue for some time unless economic growth rises substantially or the federal government increases mandates to state and local governments. This was not likely with the Republican push to pass a balanced budget initiative in 1995.

Another factor that could help boost municipal bond prices over the long term is a stabilizing of market interest rates as the Federal Reserve Board tempers its recent rate hike action. Likewise, demand for municipal bonds is unlikely to decrease without a significant reduction in taxes, another scenario not likely to materialize.

Finally, the inefficiency of the municipal bond market creates unique investment opportunities. With over 50,000 individual municipal issues, there's not an even flow of liquidity for each issue. Sudden demand for a specific issue can drive up prices rapidly, creating substantial capital gains for the fortunate holders of those bonds.

The real beauty of municipals is that you can lock in an attractive yield, benefit from their tax-favored status, and be assured of the return of principal by investing in high-grade securities.

Individual municipal bonds offer you a wide range of maturities, quality, and yields to construct the portfolio of municipals you desire. You receive semiannual income and can lock in your tax-advantaged yield, assuming you hold the bonds until maturity. Sticking with insured or top-rated municipals provides safety of principal while you clip your coupons.

When constructing your portfolio of municipal securities, it is important to remember the relationship between changes in market interest rates and the value (pricing) of existing issues trading in the secondary market. As a general rule, as market interest rates rise, the prices of existing municipals will decrease because their yield is now relatively less attractive. Conversely, as interest rates decline, the value of outstanding municipal bond issues will increase in value.

An effective way to reduce your interest rate risk and exposure to having your investments maturing at an inopportune time lies in laddering your bond maturities. In other words, you purchase bonds with maturities ranging over a period of years to prevent all your bonds coming due at one time and having to reinvest all the principal at what could be unattractive rates.

Taxing News

Before we take a look at the single state, municipal investment trust, and municipal mutual fund investment options, a word about taxes is in order. As mentioned, municipal bonds enjoy favored tax status by being exempt from federal income taxes (although municipal bond income may be subject to the alternative minimum tax). In addition, some states and localities also exempt municipal bond issues from their taxes, greatly enhancing the tax shelter.

Recent tax law changes slightly tarnished the municipal bond investment, however. Any appreciation of the principal value on municipals purchased at a discount from par value on or after May 1, 1993 is now treated as ordinary income versus capital gain status with lower tax rates. To illustrate, an investor who purchased a $10,000 municipal bond for a discounted value of $9500 will be faced with a tax liability on the $500 appreciation at higher ordinary income tax rates (depending on taxable income level), not at the lower capital gains tax rates.

Also, the "phantom income" associated with zero coupon investments needs to be considered. The interest earned on zero coupon municipal bonds is fully taxable in the year it is earned even though you do not receive any of it until the bonds mature at face value.

Individual Municipal Bond Issues

Table 5-3 lists a sampling of individual municipal bond issues from across the country to give you a flavor of the diversity of issues available for pur-

Table 5-3. Individual Municipal Bond Issues

Rating	*Issuer*	*Coupon (%)*	*Maturity*	*Yield to Maturity (%)*
AAA	Ohio Water*	5.60	6/1/02	5.10
AA–	Farmington Hills, Michigan	4.75	10/1/99	4.75
AA	Franklin City, Ohio Riverside Methodist Hospital	5.30	5/15/02	5.30
A	Colorado River* Municipal Water District	8.50	1/1/01	5.71
AAA	Sacramento* Municipal Utility District, Electricity Rev Series I	5.60	1/1/06	6.00

*MBIA-insured.

chase. Many brokerage houses publish bond recommendation lists; ask your broker to put you on its mailing list for bond recommendations.

As you can see, there's a wide variety of available municipal bonds, running the gamut from hospital to utility bonds and from general obligation various purpose to water system bonds. Before you invest, understand the specific risks of investing in each type of bond as well as the individual bond issue.

To look at one type, investors in hospital revenue bonds are well advised to assess the answers to the following pertinent questions impacting credit risk:

- *Management:* How competent is management? How good are labor relations?
- *Competition:* What is hospital's market share in relation to competitors? Does it possess any niche specialties giving it a competitive edge? How susceptible is the hospital to technological changes?
- *Market area:* How will changing demographics impact operations and profitability? What are the economic prospects of the region?
- *Facility:* How old and well maintained are the physical plant and equipment?
- *Operations:* What range of services are offered? Are staffing levels realistic? Does the hospital depend on third-party reimbursement?

- *Financial:* Is the balance sheet strong? Is cash flow increasing or decreasing? How well is debt service covered? What covenants could impair the ability to pay interest or repay the principal?

Similar types of questions should be asked for each prospective municipal bond investment and should be answered to your satisfaction. If the bond recommendation does not touch on any critical areas, request more information or find a broker who can provide the level of information required for you to make an informed decision.

When corporations issue a bond offering, they are required to make a prospectus available to potential investors. In the world of municipals, a similar document called the *official statement* is the equivalent to the corporate prospectus. Sometimes, an abbreviated form, called an *offering circular,* may take the place of the official statement. Request a copy and read it to answer your questions about the bonds, the purpose for which they are issued, and credit quality.

Municipal bond issues also come complete with a legal opinion. The legal opinion provides two major benefits for the investor. First, it assures you that the bonds represent binding obligations of the issuer according to state and local statutes. Second, it verifies whether the tax-exempt status of the interest payments is in accordance with applicable federal and local regulations.

Tapping the Hometown Advantage

Use regional brokers and their firms' research departments to narrow down the list of potential municipal bond investments that meet your investment requirements in terms of return and degree of investment risk you are willing to undertake. For example, St. Louis, Missouri–based A.G. Edwards Investments periodically publishes a *Municipal Bonds Research Report* for clients. The report covers various types of municipal bond offerings such as those of municipal electric utilities. It provides:

- A description of the issue.
- The issuing authority.
- The S&P rating outlook.
- The bond rating.
- The amount of bonds outstanding.
- The debt service coverage.

You can make an informed investment decision on the basis of such information.

Use your knowledge of the local economy and the viability of proposed projects to determine if the project revenues underpinning the municipal bond issue are assured. Or could they run into trouble with a change in the region's economic vitality?

If possible, attend public hearings discussing the bond issue and request information on the assumptions on which the projected revenues are based. In the wake of the Orange County fiasco, it's also wise to inquire about the government agency's investment posture that could influence the repayment of the municipal bond debt.

Municipal Bond Mutual Funds

Municipal bond funds come in two varieties: open-end and closed-end funds. While open-end funds trade at their net asset value (NAV), closed-end funds can trade at a premium or discount to their net asset value depending on investor sentiment and other market factors. Unlike open-end funds, closed-end mutual funds issue a set number of shares, which trade on an exchange like the New York Stock Exchange.

The attraction of closed-end funds is that the fund management does not have to sell securities out of its portfolio holdings to raise cash for share redemptions or otherwise carry a cash reserve for anticipated share redemptions. In other words, all of the fund's financial assets can be put to work in portfolio investments.

Since closed-end funds react to market mood swings, they are susceptible to wider price swings than their open-end counterparts. That creates both risk and opportunity. During the majority of 1994, many closed-end municipal bond funds traded at a discount to their NAV in the wake of a series of interest rate hikes by the Federal Reserve Board.

Some funds suffered declines in their market price of 20 percent or more. That creates opportunities for patient value hunters seeking to capitalize on an eventual closed-end municipal bond fund price rebound. This represents a strategy to seek tax-free income combined with opportunities for long-term capital gains.

Whether you invest in open- or closed-end municipal bond funds, evaluate the portfolio holdings to determine average maturity and the maturity mix as well as bond quality—to zero in on the interest rate risk and credit risk posture of the fund portfolio manager. Request a copy of the fund prospectus and a list of current holdings, and spend some time reviewing them. Don't be blindsided by funds touting higher returns but carrying higher-than-warranted interest rate and credit risks. Also, pay attention to funds bearing high expenses and 12b-1 fees that can cut into your overall return.

A List of Good Open-End Funds

There are nearly 400 municipal bond funds from which to choose appropriate investments for your portfolio. The following represent municipal bond funds with the experience, track record, and positioning to perform well given the right interest rate environment. The list includes a mix of single-state and national municipal bond funds to help you tailor your portfolio.

Fidelity Municipal Bond Fund
Telephone: 1-800-544-8888
Investment advisor: Fidelity Management and Research Co.

Net assets: $1.29 billion
Expenses: 0.49 percent
Inception: August 1976
Initial investment: $2500

Return

One-year return:	–8.61 percent through 12/31/94
Five-year return:	7.73 percent through 12/31/94
Since inception:	6.51 percent through 12/31/94

Strategy. Portfolio manager, Gary Swayze, has turned in some attractive returns with the Fidelity Municipal Bond Fund over the years. The average quality of the fund stands at AA, with nearly 90 percent of the portfolio rate A or higher.

Swayze also seeks out undervalued situations such as health care issues, California municipals, and electric utilities that can benefit from a more realistic appraisal in the market.

Though the longer average maturity (around 19 years) than many other municipal funds may cause more volatility, Swayze has proven adept at delivering in all types of economic and interest rate environments.

Flagship All-American Tax Exempt A
Telephone: 1-800-227-4648
Investment advisor: Flagship Financial, Inc.
Net assets: $188 million
Expenses: 0.65 percent
Inception: October 1988
Initial investment: $3000

Return

One-year return:	−5.89 percent through 12/31/94
Five-year return:	7.57 percent through 12/31/94
Since inception:	8.11 percent through 12/31/94

Strategy. The Flagship All-American Tax-Exempt A Fund has delivered consistently strong returns through the end of 1993. Portfolio manager, Robert Ashbauch, has been restructuring his mix as of 1995 with industrial development and pollution control bonds taking on a heavier weighting, while education and utility bonds are becoming a smaller part of the portfolio. The current lull in return will be temporary. Purchase this fund for solid long-term performance.

Medalist Virginia Municipal Bond Fund
Telephone: 1-800-723-9512
Investment advisor: Signet Asset Management
Net assets: $68.5 million
Expenses: 0.75 percent
Inception: October 1990
Initial investment: $1000

Return

Annualized total return:	5.72 percent through 9/30/94 since inception
One-year return:	−6.21 percent through 9/30/94

Strategy. The Medalist Virginia Municipal Bond Fund invests at least 65 percent of its assets in Virginia municipal bonds with the goal that:

- *Either* at least 80 percent of its annual interest income is exempt from federal regular and Virginia state income taxes.
- *Or* at least 80 percent of its net assets are invested in obligations whose interest income is exempt from federal regular and Virginia state income taxes.

It invests only in investment-grade debt securities at the time of purchase.

Nuveen Tax-Free California Insured
Telephone: 1-800-621-7227
Investment advisor: Nuveen Advisory Corp.
Net assets: $194 million
Expenses: 0.71 percent
Inception: July 1986
Initial investment: $1000

Return

One-year return:	–6.91 percent through 12/31/94
Five-year return:	6.34 percent through 12/31/94
Since inception:	6.51 percent through 12/31/94

Strategy. The Nuveen Tax-Free California Insured Fund purchases California municipal obligations that are either covered by insurance guaranteeing the timely payment of principal and interest or backed by an escrow or trust account containing sufficient U.S. government or U.S. government agency securities to ensure the timely payment of principal and interest.

Fund management takes a value approach, searching out investment-grade undervalued or underrated California municipal obligations.

United Municipal High-Income Fund
Telephone: 1-800-366-5465
Investment advisor: Waddell & Reed Investment Management
Net assets: $322 million
Expenses: 0.71 percent
Inception: January 1986
Initial investment: $500

Return

One-year return:	–7.23 percent through 12/31/94
Five-year return:	+6.76 percent through 12/31/94

Strategy. The United Municipal High Income Fund seeks high income by means of a concentration (around 75 percent) of nonrated municipal bond issues. The nonrated strategy is based on the fund management's ability to garner higher yields coupled with better call protection. The high yield emphasis targets superior performance in both rising and declining interest rate scenarios.

To date, the fund has performed well over the long term, and offers an interesting choice for investors willing to take on a bit more risk.

Vanguard New York Insured Tax-Free
Telephone: 1-800-662-7447
Investment advisor: Vanguard Group

Net assets: $816 million
Expenses: 0.19 percent
Inception: April 1986
Initial investment: $3000

Return

One-year return:	–5.63 percent through 12/31/94
Five-year return:	7.01 percent through 12/31/94
Since inception	6.61 percent through 12/31/94

Strategy. The Vanguard New York Insured Tax-Free Fund purchases insured New York municipal obligations. Fund management strives to achieve stable and predictable tax-exempt income flow by purchasing call-protected securities. The fund managers are not adverse to raising fund liquidity to reduce risk.

Taking the insured route, the fund's quality averages AAA, with 97 percent of the fund portfolio rated AAA. This fund has ranked in the top 10 percent of New York State municipal funds and has outperformed the Lehman Municipal Index for the past five years.

... And in the Closed-End Arena

Thomas J. Herzfeld is president of Thomas J. Herzfeld Advisors, Inc. and publisher of *The Closed-End Fund Research Report* and *The Investor's Guide to Closed-End Funds.* (Both can be ordered by contacting Thomas J. Herzfeld Advisors, Inc., The Herzfeld Building, P.O. Box 161465, Miami, FL 33116, 305-271-1900.) Herzfeld says there's something for everyone in the closed-end fund municipal market. Investment options include leveraged and nonleveraged, state and national, insured and noninsured, investment-grade and junk, intermediate and other maturities, and single-industry municipal bond funds.

"We use a strategy of purchasing a basketful of closed-end municipal bond funds with wide discounts. We hold them for income and then trade them for short-term capital gains when the discount narrows, reinvesting our funds into other municipal funds priced at large discounts. This works to keep our risk posture low while generating income and capital gains," says Herzfeld.

Municipal Unit Trusts

A new wrinkle to investing in tax-free municipal bonds deserves some consideration. The *unit investment trust* (*UIT*) is a fixed portfolio of professionally selected fixed-income securities. By purchasing units in the trust, you avoid the hassle of selecting and monitoring your own portfolio of individual municipal securities.

Nuveen & Company, Van Kampen Merritt, and others offer both national and state UITs, typically sold in units of 10 ($1000) or 50 ($5000). The benefits include professional expertise, diversification at a reasonable cost (UIT expenses usually come in around 0.15 percent, compared with 0.75 percent or more for municipal bond mutual funds), and a fairly predictable stream of tax-free income for a decade or more.

With a fixed portfolio reflecting each security, yield, maturity, credit rating, and call features, investors know exactly what they are purchasing. The trust distributes the municipal bond interest until all the bonds mature or are called. Check the prospectus to see if the estimated long-term return matches your monthly tax-exempt income requirements.

Two caveats: First, make sure you plan to hold the UIT long term, or the approximate 4 percent sales load could cut deep into any short-term income. Second, the UIT industry does not publish any performance statistics; so comparison shopping is a bit more difficult than for mutual funds.

Municipal investments can deliver the security and the return you desire, but you need to investigate before you invest. To help you in that regard, I recommend the *Lynch Municipal Bond Advisory,* an independent investment newsletter written by James Lynch, a 35-year municipal bond market veteran writing for the individual investor.

The newsletter keeps subscribers informed on municipal bond investment strategies, recommended new issues, comparative yields with U.S. Treasuries, model portfolios for investors from different states, and economic analysis. The annual subscription rate is $250. For information, contact Lynch Municipal Bond Advisory, Inc., P.O. Box 20476, New York, NY 10025, 212-663-5552.

6
Tracking Initial Public Offerings (IPOs)

Coming to Market: The Role of IPOs

Initial public offerings represent just what their name implies: the initial offering of a company's stock to the general public. (In the next chapter, we will discuss opportunities in private placements of company stock and other similar investment options.)

One of the major attractions of IPOs lies in the fact that the initial offering price may be set too low in relation to the company's market niche, management talent, and future prospects. Along those same lines, the market may recognize the company's prospects and create additional demand for the stock, sending the company's stock price immediately skyrocketing.

You only need to look back to the Boston Chicken, Inc. IPO to see their opportunities and associated risks. The franchise food company came to market in late 1993 priced at $10 per share (adjusted for a 2-for-1 stock split in November 1994). Intense public interest in the stock made Boston Chicken's stock price take flight, soaring 143 percent over its initial offering price, opening up at $22⅝ per share and closing at $24¼ per share for the day. Ultimately, Boston Chicken's stock price climbed to $25½ per share before the end of 1993, more than two and a half times its stated offering price.

Obviously, investors fortunate enough to get in on the Boston Chicken IPO in its early stages profited handsomely. Certainly any investor would love to be involved with an IPO as successful as Boston Chicken. However, there's the risk of jumping on the bandwagon too late. You'll see that when we get to the current review of Boston Chicken, in the analysis section near the end of this chapter.

The hometown investor has a distinct advantage over other investors in the IPO market. As a resident of the area in which the upcoming IPO first initiates operations, you can see first-hand how well the company and its management run the business. In the case of Boston Chicken, hometown investors can actually drive up to the restaurants and taste the chicken and other menu offerings. They can also get a feel for customer traffic and the growing popularity of the place.

In addition, management is not a just a list of names in a prospectus. More likely, hometown investors know some of the management team or board of directors members either personally or through business associates. The local and regional business press also comes into play with more in-depth coverage of the firm and its owners than the national media would offer.

Investors in Massachusetts were very familiar with Boston Chicken. The first restaurant opened in Newton, Massachusetts in 1985, nearly ten years before the firm's initial public offering. The company's track record was already firmly in place. Their strategy of wholesome meals was working, and the company turned a profit in 1993 after several years of losses. Equally important, in late 1991 and 1992, outside investors took control of the company and brought in top management talent from top-quality food service operators.

All this combined to increase investor interest. Feverish investors anxious to get on the Boston Chicken Express bid the price of its shares to unsustainable lofty levels. Investors who purchased the company's stock late in the game (in this case only a matter of weeks after the IPO) around the $25½-per-share level saw their investment value plummet to $16⅛ per share in 1994 before rebounding a tad.

Although many large investors were able to buy the offering at $10 per share, most small investors could not get a piece of the action until after the stock's meteoric rise. Likewise, company officers purchased 900,000 restricted shares at $20 per share that couldn't be sold for 180 days. Even more to the point, pre-IPO investors in the company had paid only an average of $2.97 per share according to the prospectus. Obviously, some Boston Chicken investors did very well indeed, while other Boston Chicken IPO investors got their investment feathers plucked.

The point is that the hometown investor has an edge on the information pipeline and the opportunity to subscribe to shares early, before the price gets run up to lofty levels. Keeping in touch with local and area business developments through the local media, business contacts, and personal observation can give you a jump on other investors and put you in line for substantial investment profits.

Maintaining close contact with your regional broker will keep you aware of upcoming IPOs and provide you with an honest appraisal of the management team and the firm's prospects. Staying in touch with local university people can also put you onto the trail of potential IPOs and private placements. (Many fledgling firms originate or operate out of university and college research efforts, entrepreneurial centers, or technology transfer centers.)

IPO Performance

There have been a number of extremely successful IPOs in recent years. Many well-known companies such as Circus Circus Enterprises, Inc., EXEL Limited, The Home Depot, Inc., Microsoft Corporation, and Stewart Enterprises have gone public since the eighties. Table 6-1 shows the IPO performance of a number of companies to illustrate the investment gains potential in ferreting out the right IPOs. As you can see from the table, IPOs come from a wide variety of industries and thus offer plenty of opportunities for diversification.

From an academic standpoint, a 1991 IPO study by Jay Ritter, an associate professor of finance at the University of Illinois, concluded that for the first three years after going public, IPOs, on average, generated a total return to shareholders of around 34.5 percent. In comparison, comparable established companies earned an average total return approaching 62 percent.

Of course, those IPO numbers are clouded by the number of IPOs that do not perform well and by the fact that the failure rate for IPOs, compared to that of established companies, is quite high, just by the nature

Table 6-1. IPO Performance*

Company	*Industry*	*IPO price ($)*	*IPO date*	*High price ($)*
Circus Circus	Gaming	2.03	10/25/83	49¾
EXEL Ltd.	Insurance	25.50	7/18/91	52¼
Home Depot	Building supply	.19	9/22/81	51½
Microsoft	Computer software	1.19	3/13/86	65¼

*All prices adjusted for stock splits.

of fledgling businesses. Of course, not all IPOs are solid winners, but the ones that are stand to outperform the market averages by substantial margins.

Another study by Professor Robert Jennings of the University of Indiana and Professor Christopher Barry of Texas Christian University found that, on average, 90 percent of the initial day's mean return gets earned on the opening transaction. You don't want to chase an IPO stock only to establish a loss as the stock settles down after an initial surge.

Just as there are right IPOs to invest in, there are right market cycles when IPO investing makes more sense than at other times. During IPO market booms, market prices tend to get distorted in comparison to a fair presentation of the firm's underlying prospects. Investors—anxious to get in on the big winner—bid up prices to lofty, often unsustainable, levels.

Be wary of frenzied IPO markets and avoid chasing an IPO beyond reasonable valuations. On the other side of the coin, during slack IPO markets, brokers may be calling you with "hot" IPO deals. Remember, "hot" deals can burn you. Slow IPO markets can also spell opportunity as market inefficiencies create initial prices that may be too low in light of the company prospects.

Investor's Business Daily's New Issues Index tracks IPOs for 12-month price performance. After the hot IPO markets of 1992 and 1993, the postoffering gain by all IPOs declined over 30 percent from January 1994 to mid-June 1994.

Since the most attractive IPOs are typically oversubscribed, an unsolicited call from a broker about an upcoming IPO should serve as a warning shot across the bow. Furthermore, a reduced issue price can signal an unattractive market environment (little secondary market interest to support the stock price) or declining interest in the issue.

A rise in the price of the expected offering price and an increase in the number of shares planned to be offered bode well for the offering, since a surge in investor demand typically pushes up the offering price dramatically. The hope is that investor enthusiasm will carry over into the aftermarket and continue to propel the company's stock price higher.

Beware of sweeteners used to entice investors to otherwise unattractive IPOs. These can come in the form of a warrant attached to each share of stock or a preferred issue giving the purchaser special rights.

Recognize the risks associated with developmental stage companies without a track record or proven products or service. Many of these companies bite the dust before turning a profit. Of course, there are significant investment gain opportunities in biomedical or biotechnolgy new issues, but you must be prepared to accept a higher degree of risk.

Ascertain how the issue is being underwritten. A best efforts underwriter does not have to absorb any unsold shares and does not guarantee a 100 percent sale of all shares offered. The underwriter limits its own risk and may have less incentive to support the stock in the aftermarket.

Most IPO deals are backed by the underwriter taking responsibility and the risk for selling out the issue. This means that slow selling issues can be backed by a high-pressure sales effort to unload the stock. Remember, investigate before you invest. Refer to the following discussion on what to look for in an IPO prospectus.

If you are fortunate enough to purchase at the offering price and the stock jumps 20 percent or more on the opening, it may be a wise move to sell. After all, more than a 20 percent gain is nothing to be ashamed of. Generally, there will be some initial downside price pressure as flippers (traders who immediately sell and take their gain) bail out. If the stock's price level seems to hold its own under high volume, it's a good sign and it may be best to hang on for additional gains.

Brokerage firms discourage flippers; some even go so far as taking away commissions on stock that has been flipped. So you have to weigh your potential gain from flipping a specific IPO as opposed to not getting invited back to the party by that broker.

So what's the best way to play the IPO market without getting burned? Without a doubt, developing a pipeline into the IPO information network is a must. To remain a viable player in the IPO market, the individual investor must maintain a steady flow of information about upcoming issues with the potential to outperform the market in the days, weeks, and months ahead.

"Keep in regular contact with your smaller regional underwriters. They always tend to get a piece of the action and are more than willing to work with new clients," advises Robert E. Mescal, research analyst for *New Issues,* published by The Institute for Econometric Research in Fort Lauderdale, Florida.

Request a copy of the underwriting calendar your broker's firm will participate in over the near future. Then request a copy of the prospectus (red herring) of the ones you are interested in learning more about. New issues cannot be sold without the broker first providing the investor with a prospectus.

Of course, it's still a matter of economics. IPOs are one way for brokers to reward clients who generate handsome commissions in their accounts. If you don't do a fair amount of business with your broker, don't be expected to be invited to the IPO party. After all, available shares in any given IPO are limited.

Potential IPO investors can establish a track record with an underwriter during slack times and help ensure themselves a piece of the IPO action when the market improves and demand rises for IPO shares. Simply put, you need to generate commission revenues for your broker to get informed about new offerings.

"If you can't get in on the initial offering, wait for the aftermarket to see how prices shake out. If the company's underlying fundamentals are strong and the stock appears to be reasonably valued, purchase it in the aftermarket," says Mescal.

Investigate Before You Invest

"Without a doubt, the number one rule before investing in any IPO is to study, not just read, the red herring (prospectus). If you don't understand parts of the prospectus, have someone explain it to you until you do," advises Mescal.

According to Mescal, some important points to look out for include the number of shares offered and the origin of those shares. For example, suppose 1 million shares are being offered to the public and 350,000 of those shares are being offered by company management. Only 65 percent of the net proceeds of the stock offering will be available to the company for operations. The other 35 percent goes directly into the pockets of management as they sell off a portion of their company ownership.

Has management and the board kept a substantial interest in the firm so that its success has a direct impact on their own wealth? If so, that's a positive sign. On the other hand, if a high percentage of insiders are selling large portions of their company stock, it may be a warning sign that they are getting out while the getting is good. There may be valid reasons why some management team members are selling their shares but a wholesale unloading of company stock should be viewed with a cautious eye.

Likewise, IPO investors need to analyze the company's line of business. Check into how other industry companies are performing. Ask yourself, is the market already saturated? Or does this company possess products or services that can carve out a successful market niche? Investigate the company's track record to see how well it has performed in different economic scenarios. Who are the company's major customers and competitors? Are a majority of the company's anticipated revenues heavily dependent on just a few customers? For example, if the company's largest customers operate in the defense industry and major defense cutbacks loom, what are the firms' true prospects in the years ahead?

Review the section termed Certain Factors or Investment Considerations, which spells out specific risks such as heavy reliance on one or two top management personnel, dependence on raw materials from a sole source, intense industry competition, and high leverage and debt levels.

The Use of Proceeds section lays out how the company intends to use the net proceeds of the public stock offering. Will the funds be used to just pay down debt, or will they be put to use expanding product line, increasing market share, or building new facilities?

Next, pay attention to the company's financials. Have earnings been consistent and growing? Will the company's debt level negatively impact operations and place a heavy interest payment burden that may be hard to meet during economic contractions? Calculate the price/earnings ratio using the income figures in the red herring and the expected offering price: Does the company's anticipated price/earnings ratio fall in line with industry norms? Is the price/earnings ratio reasonable based on past growth rates?

Assess the company's operations and marketing strategies to determine if they are realistic in light of projected economic scenarios and the level of competition it is likely to encounter. Are they realistic or pie in the sky?

Management is the key to any successful business venture. Review management's track record and expertise in the industry. Does the management team possess sufficient industry and management experience? Or is management top heavy in technical expertise and woefully lacking in management talent? Often, the entrepreneurs or technicians that create a business or product do not have the wherewithal to develop succesful marketing and operating strategies. Look for a well balanced, seasoned management team with experience in key management functions.

Finally, a study by Professor Roni Michaely at Cornell University indicates that it's wise to pay attention to which investment banking firm is handling the underwriting. Michaely ranked 179 new issue underwriters, using size as a proxy for reputation, with 23 qualifying as "prestigious." He discovered a profound difference between the IPOs issued by the 23 prestigious investment bankers and those issued by less prestigious firms. IPOs issued by prestigious firms performed significantly better in the market. As a general rule, the prestigious underwriters can afford to discriminate and take the better issues to market.

IPO Information Sources

A wealth of IPO information sources are available to the individual investor seeking to capitalize on upcoming IPOs. Many sources can be accessed through your city or university library, or you may subscribe to publications and study them at your own convenience.

The financial press, including such publications as *Fortune* and *Forbes,* routinely covers initial public offerings in articles. In addition, more frequent business publications cover the IPO market with regular columns. *Barron's* reports on IPOs in its Offerings in the Offing portion of the "Market Laboratory" section. *Investor's Business Daily*'s New Issues Pipeline highlights recent IPOs, while its Financing Business/New Issues section provides prices of current IPOs. And the *Security Traders Handbook* carries a regular column, New Issue Informer, which provides information from the red herrings of forthcoming IPOs.

Subscription information for *Barron's, Investor's Business Daily,* and *Security Traders Handbook* is as follows:

Barron's
The Dow Jones Business and Financial Weekly
200 Burnett Road
P.O. Box 7014
Chicopee, MA 01021-9901
Annual subscription: $129
13-week trial offer: $34
1-800-328-6800, ext. 456

Investor's Business Daily
Customer Service Department A
P.O. Box 66370
Los Angeles, CA 90066-0370
Annual subscription: $169
6 months: $94
1-800-306-9744

Security Traders Handbook
Bay Tact Corporation
440 Route 198
Woodstock Valley, CT 06282
Annual subscription: $60
1-800-426-6825

For more indepth information and analysis of IPOs, take a look at the following investment newsletters.

New Issue Digest. Now in its twenty-fifth year of continued publication, *New Issue Digest* profiles upcoming IPOs and adds an Editor's Note highlighting key issues related to the offering. For example, the Editor's Note on Investment Technology Group, Inc. stated that "immediately prior to the offering, Investment Technology Group will issue 15,000,000 shares of common stock to Jeffries Group in exchange for all shares of ITG that Jeffries holds... . Jeffries Group will own about 82% of Investment Technology's shares after the offering." The newsletter does not make specific recommendations but provides an objective analysis of the IPO from which individual investors can base their investment decisions.

New Issue Digest discusses industry trends and provides an update of earnings, growth rates, price/sales ratios, revenues, and stock market prices of companies listed in the investment newsletter and traded for less than 18 months.

New Issue Digest is a supplement to *Growth Stock Outlook* (GSO) and included in the subscription price of GSO. GSO can be ordered by contacting Growth Stock Outlook, Inc., P.O. Box 15381, Chevy Chase, MD 20825 ,or call 301-654-5205. The annual subscription rate is $195.

New Issues. *New Issues* provides new issue purchase recommendations backed by a comprehensive analysis of the stock. It also points out new issues offerings to avoid. The newsletter's Calendar of Forthcoming Offerings details every forthcoming initial public stock offering; so you can be assured you won't miss any attractive opportunities. It continuously monitors all previous buy recommendations until a sell recommendation has been issued. The Featured Aftermarket Buy section recommends secondary market buying opportunities on attractively priced IPOs.

You can subscribe to *New Issues* by contacting The Institute for Econometric Research, 3471 North Federal, Fort Lauderdale, FL 33306-9989, or call 1-800-442-9000. A regular annual subscription rate is $200, but *New Issues* offers a special one-year subscription for only $95 and an introductory six-month trial for $55. Annual subscribers receive a complimentary copy of *Stock Market Logic,* a perennial best selling investment book by Norman Fosback. The subscription price also includes the Weekly Action Line Telephone Service.

Emerging & Special Situations. Standard & Poor's *Emerging & Special Situations* represents another excellent source of new issue information. This newsletter profiles new issues that hold promise for the future. An annual subscription runs $241, and a three-month trial subscription costs $60. To obtain information, call 800-221-5277 or write to Standard & Poor's, 25 Broadway, New York, NY 10004.

IPO Success Stories and Aftermarket Considerations

As Mescal indicated, if you happen to miss getting in on an IPO before it hits the street, it's not too late to get in on future potential gains.

New Issues covered Baby Superstore, Inc. in its August 17, 1994 publication. The stock was scheduled to come to market at an offering price between $15 and $17 per share in September 1994. The stock hit the street at $31¼ and surged to a high of $61¼ per share before settling back to the $54¼-per-share level in mid-February 1995.

New Issues recommended Adtran, Inc. at its offering price between $14 and $16 per share. The stock opened at $20⅝ per share in August 1994 and reached a high of $53 per share before retreating a tad to around $50 per share in mid-February 1995.

OfficeMax was featured in the September 16, 1994 *New Issues* but failed to garner an outright recommendation. The fact that Kmart will reap all the benefits of the offering with none going to the new public company may have had a factor in the no "recommendation" decision. Be that as it may, OfficeMax was slated to come to market between $16 and $19 per share. In actuality, the stock opened on the New York Stock Exchange at $23 per share, rose to $27⅝ per share in early 1995 before retreating a little to $25¾ in mid-February 1995.

Here's an updated investment perspective of these companies for the aftermarket investor.

Baby Superstore, Inc.
1201 Woods Chapel Road
Duncan, NC 29334

Stock exchange: NASDAQ
Ticker symbol: BSST
Telephone: 803-968-9292

Industry Review. Overall demographics are not as favorable as Baby Superstore's growth prospects. According to the National Center of Health Statistics, U.S. births have declined from 4.1 million in 1991 and 1992 to only 3.9 million in 1993. However, industry consolidation means well positioned players are targeted to increase market share. Price competition is intense in the industry.

Company Profile. Baby Superstore, Inc. operates a chain of 43 baby and children product superstores in 13 states. Its average retail outlet covers some 22,000 square feet, with newer stores averaging between 30,000 and 45,000 square feet. The company targets increased market share by focusing on metropolitan areas with populations of 400,000 or more. The product line includes a broad assortment of high-quality, brand name baby-related products at everyday low prices, typically 10 to 30 percent below department store prices.

Proceeds of the offering were scheduled to fuel expansion plans for 11 new superstores in the remainder of 1994 and another 10 to 15 new stores in 1995. This follows on the heels of an already aggressive expansion campaign. Over the past five years, the number of superstores grew in excess of 55 percent. The company operates mainly in the southeastern and midwest markets.

Management Talent. Chief Executive Officer Jack P. Tate owned over 54 percent of the outstanding common stock after the IPO and has a significant stake in the success of the business. He has served as CEO since founding the company in 1970 and has been the Chairman of the Board of Directors since 1988. President Linda M. Robertson has served in that capacity since 1993 and as Chief Operating Officer since the company was founded.

In recent years, the company has beefed up its financial expertise with new hires from outside the firm and the addition of outside directors from the finance community.

Financial Status. The company has adequate working capital and no long-term debt to burden operations and earnings. The expansion program will put a damper on earnings since Baby Superstore writes off all costs associated with new store openings as incurred. Even so, company profits for the third quarter of fiscal 1994 surged 40 percent on a 65 percent rise in revenues.

Particular Strengths. Twenty years of experience in the baby products business means the company has staying power and talented management in a cost-competitive environment. The rollout of new stores will keep Baby Superstore revenues and earnings growth on track for the foreseeable future. Concentration on maintaining its low operating cost structure is a key ingredient in the Baby Superstore success story.

Financial Statistics

($ millions except per-share data)

	Fiscal year ended		
	1/27/93	*1/26/94*	*1/25/95*
Revenues	63	104	175
Net income (loss)	1.5	3.8	7.1
Earnings (loss)/share	.15	.38	.44
Dividend/share	—	—	—
Long-term debt	4.9	12	—
Stock price range/share:			1994
High			47¼
Low			18

Investment Assessment. Baby Superstore, Inc. is on a fast track to market expansion and increased market share. While near-term gross margins and earnings per share will be held back by new store openings and price reductions, the long-term picture is bright. The company is craftily employing Wal-Mart Stores' tried and true expansion strategy. Look for dramatically improved earnings as the company nears completion of its present expansion policy.

Assuming the absence of a bear market, the company's improving profit picture should be rewarded with higher stock prices and price/earnings multiples. Baby Superstore represents a solid growth opportunity for the patient investor.

ADTRAN, Inc.
901 Explorer Boulevard
Huntsville, AL 35806-2807

Stock exchange: NASDAQ
Ticker symbol: ADTN
Telephone: 205-971-8000

Industry Review. ADTRAN, Inc. operates in the communications industry, providing high-speed digital transmission voice and data communications products to telephone companies and businesses. The rapid change in the telecommunications industry has spawned new markets for innovative companies on the cutting edge of technology. With the spread of personal computers and modems, the move by telecommunications companies to provide interactive product options through the telephone line opens up tremendous market opportunities.

Worldwide demand for enhanced telecommunications products promises to accelerate as we move toward the twenty-first century. Companies that can provide dependable, high-quality telecommunications devices and service will carve out market share and high profits.

Company Profile. ADTRAN, Inc. designs, develops, manufactures, and markets a broad range of high-speed digital (state-of-the-art) telecommunication products utilized by telephone companies and businesses. It also customizes its products for private label distribution and for original equipment manufacturers (OEM) to incorporate into their own products.

ADTRAN's line of over 200 products centers around a core technology serving the local loop and central office digital communications market. Its revenues are derived from three market sectors: local loop and central office (59.1 percent), OEM products (27.4 percent), and customer premises equipment (CPE) (13.5 percent).

The company's broad customer base includes all seven Baby Bells, the three largest interexchange carriers, many of the 1300 independent telephone companies, and a multitude of worldwide communications, electronics, and industrial companies. The Baby Bells account for approximately 47 percent of annual ADTRAN revenues.

Revenues nearly quadrupled between 1989 and 1993, while net income almost tripled. Revenues in 1994 easily broke the $100 million mark for the first time in the company's history, coming in at $123 million.

The company serves the international market through a combination of direct sales and distribution agreements. Through 1993, international sales revenues contributed only 1 percent of annual revenues and represent a major market segment not yet tapped by the company.

Management Talent. Cofounder Mark C. Smith has served as Chairman, President, and Chief Executive Officer since the company began operations in January 1986. All the top management team members possess extensive telecommunications and information system industry experience, both with the company and with other industry firms such as Motorola, Universal Data Systems (also cofounded by Smith), Paradyne Corporation, SCI Systems, Inc. and AMBAC, Inc. In August 1994, ADTRAN beefed up its manufacturing expertise by bringing on board a Vice President of Manufacturing with full operations responsibility for a division of Exide Electronics, Inc. Top management owns in excess of 50 percent of the company's outstanding stock.

Financial Status. The company is plush with over $60 million in working capital (including over $8 million in short-term investments) and completely free of long-term debt.

Particular Strengths. Strong earnings and cash flow will keep capital flowing to research and development efforts, the lifeblood of the company. Fully 25 percent of ADTRAN's employees work on product development programs. The company nearly doubled its research and development expenditures between 1991 and 1993 and expended nearly $14 million in 1994, an almost 40 percent increase over 1993's level.

After paying off revenue bonds used to finance the company's headquarters and manufacturing facilities, over $8 million of the proceeds from the stock offering will be used for product development and expansion of sales and marketing activities.

The company targets reducing the product development cost of each succeeding product generation and then lowering its price to gain additional market share.

Financial Statistics

($ millions except per-share data)

	1992	1993	1994
Revenues	57	72	123
Net income (loss)	8.7	8.5	18.6
Earnings (loss)/share	.51	.50	1.03
Dividend/share	—	—	—
Long-term debt	6.5	10.1	—
Stock price range/share:			1994
High			46¾
Low			18

Investment Assessment. ADTRAN achieved record results for 1994 with a better than 70 percent increase in revenues and more than a doubling of earnings. New product introductions in each of the company's three operating segments during recent quarters promise future revenue and earnings increases.

The company already commands the leading market share in the local loop and central office digital transmission product segment. With increased product development geared to tap the explosive business and consumer markets, ADTRAN is poised to continue its impressive growth.

OfficeMax, Inc.
3605 Warrensville Center Road
Shaker Heights, OH 44122

Stock exchange: NYSE
Ticker symbol: OMX
Telephone: 216-921-6900

Industry Review. OfficeMax, Inc. competes against such office supply industry giants as Office Depot, Inc. and Staples, Inc., as well as warehouse clubs with office supply sectors such as Wal-Mart Stores' Sam's Club.

The office supplies industry is undergoing a major consolidation across the country with the small, local, mom-and-pop office supply and stationery stores losing market share to the low-priced superstore chains.

Despite the proliferation of superstores, there's still plenty of room for major industry players to garner market share away from their smaller and financially weaker competitors.

Company Profile. OfficeMax, Inc. ranks as the second largest office supply retailer (behind Office Depot, Inc.) with more than 345 office products superstores spanning nearly 40 states. It offers a wide variety of quality brand name and private label products at prices generally 30 to 70 percent below manufacturers' suggested retail and catalog prices. The company's stores sport some 6000 products, giving the firm's customers a wide variety of items not typically found in more traditional office supply stores, warehouse clubs, and mass merchandise outlets.

The company's expansion strategy is two-pronged with chain acquisitions and new store development combining to expand its network of outlets. The company plans to open 70 new superstores annually over the next three years.

OfficeMax supplies its stores with merchandise out of a number of warehouse and delivery distribution centers strategically located across the nation.

Management Talent. Cofounder Michael Feuer serves as a company Director, President, and Chief Executive Officer. The top management team has been compiled since 1990 with executives lured away from a wide variety of firms with national retail operations such as Wal-Mart Stores, Inc., Zayre Corporation, Fabri-Centers of America, Inc., Federated Department Stores, Inc., and Biz-Mart, Inc.

Financial Status. OfficeMax, Inc. has plenty of working capital and cash flow to fund its aggressive expansion strategy. The company turned the corner and posted a tripling of revenues and a profit of 16 cents per share for fiscal year ended January 22, 1994, after two consecutive losing years.

Particular Strengths. The company has a 22 percent interest in Corporate Express, and is using its relationship with that company to help further penetrate the corporate office supplies market segment. The two companies cooperate in merchandise purchasing and information systems expertise.

With the typical OfficeMax superstore open less than an average of two years, increased market potential in existing markets has yet been tapped to its full potential. Anticipated increases in same-store sales, coupled with the addition of 70 new stores a year, will boost the company's market share in the years ahead as the fragmented office supplies industry consolidates.

Financial Statistics

($ million except per-share data)

	Fiscal year ended		
	1/23/93	1/22/94	1/22/95
Revenues	528	1422	1841
Net income (loss)	(.8)	10.8	30.4
Earnings (loss)/share	—	.21	.60
Dividend/share	—	—	—
Long-term debt	28	28	29
Stock price range/share:			1994
High			26½
Low			21⅝

Investment Assessment. OfficeMax is close on the heels of Office Depot in terms of store and revenue growth, but has yet to prove itself in terms of consistent earnings. With both stocks trading in the $20–$30-per-share range, it doesn't take a brain surgeon to plunk down his or her money on the proven ability of Office Depot to generate dependable earnings. However, a smart investor would keep a watchful eye on OfficeMax and its stock price. Purchase on price weakness coupled with several quarters in a row of improved profit performance.

Boston Chicken, Inc.*
14103 Denver West Parkway
P.O. Box 4086
Golden, CO 80401-4086

Stock exchange: NASDAQ
Ticker symbol: BOST
Telephone: 303-278-9500

Industry Review. Boston Chicken, Inc. operates in the highly competitive franchise food industry against such major players as McDonald's, Applebee's, Pepsi's Pizza Hut, Burger King, Wendy's, and, in head-to-head competition, Kentucky Fried Chicken, Kenny Rogers' Roasters, and other chicken franchises. Changing consumer tastes and health con-

*The company changed its stores' name to Boston Market, Inc. in 1995 to reflect its expanding menu.

sciousness have given way to more wholesome meals from the traditional fast food chains and the industry as a whole.

Company Profile. Boston Chicken, Inc. features fresh and wholesome meals teamed up with the convenience and full food value concept of the popular fast food chain restaurants. The first Boston Chicken restaurant opened in 1985. Since then, the company has expanded to a network of 534 restaurants in 30 states and the District of Columbia at the end of fiscal 1994. The firm anticipates operating over 1000 stores within three years.

Expansion is based on penetrating a market through the use of the area developer concept (ADI) with experienced multiunit food service operators. This promises to deliver economies of scale in television advertising, employee training, and store support activities while focusing on better customer service and store operations.

Management Talent. Boston Chicken has compiled a capable team of retail and food service industry veterans. Chairman and Chief Executive Officer Scott A. Beck leads a young, aggressive management group mostly in their thirties and forties. Top executives were enticed away from such successful firms as Blockbuster, Bennigan's Restaurants, Burger King, Quaker Oats, KFC National Management, and Chili's, Inc.

Financial Status. After going public in November 1993, Boston Chicken floated another stock offering in August 1994 with the nearly $106 million in net proceeds slated for store development and partial financing of area developers to gain further market penetration. Part of the proceeds will be used to bolster restaurant support operations and paying down its revolving credit line.

The company had working capital in excess of $27 million at the end of fiscal 1994 and $130 in 4½ percent convertible subordinated debt due 2004. The long-term debt carries a conversion price of $55.938 per share.

Particular Strengths. Strong store expansion will feed growing franchise fees and increase market penetration. The ADI strategy targets economies of scale and more efficient operations in a given market area, providing the company's franchises with a competitive edge.

Financial Statistics

($ millions except per-share data)

	Fiscal year ended		
	12/27/92	12/26/93	12/25/94
Revenues	8.3	42.5	96.1
Net income (loss)	(6.3)	1.6	16.2
Earnings (loss)/share	(.41)	.06	.38
Dividend/share	—	—	—
Long-term debt	—	—	130
Stock price range/share:		1993	1994
High		25½	24¼
Low		17¾	13½

Investment Assessment. It's important to note that Boston Chicken's significant earnings per-share surge occurred despite a better than 31 percent increase in the number of outstanding shares of common stock. Look for continued revenues and earnings-per-share growth as the expansion plans move forward and additional stores come on stream.

However, it always makes good sense to evaluate a potential investment based on a review of the firm's underlying value and prospects in relation to its current market price. Since its public offering in November 1993 and secondary stock sales in August 1994, the market price of Boston Chicken stock has treaded in a relatively narrow range failing to break out over the $25-per-share level.

"Boston Chicken's a classic case of overvaluation at the onset. High institutional interest in the company drove demand for the stock and the price higher than warranted. The individual investor could not get a piece of the Boston Chicken offering before it hit the market," says Charles Allmon, editor of *New Issue Digest*.

Even though the stock had dropped to new lows below $15 per share, Allmon still considers Boston Chicken too high priced. Only after the stock retreats to its initial offering price of $10 per share will Allmon consider the stock worthy of a look for possible investment.

The Short Selling Option

"The current IPO market is the most dangerous I have seen in 25 years of tracking the new issues segment," warns Allmon.

According to Allmon, there are still opportunities for getting in on fairly valued IPOs with great prospects, but he's been sitting on the sidelines waiting for the right stock and market conditions.

In the meantime, the high institutional interest driving up IPO prices lends itself to short selling opportunities to capitalize on overpriced situations poised to come crashing down as reality sets in.

Allmon uses the price/sales ratio as one indicator of fair valuation and as a way to ferret out overpriced IPOs. "IPOs with sales/price ratios running above the 6 level could see their prices dropping 50% to 75%," says Allmon.

That's where strategic short selling could improve your investment performance in a difficult market. As explained in Chap. 4, short selling consists of selling stock you don't own (you borrow it from your broker for a fee) at a high price only to replace it later with stock purchased after the stock prices drops.

When assessing whether to purchase long or short sell your hometown IPOs, remember to put the investment in proper perspective. Analyze the investment in light of anticipated local, regional, and national economic scenarios, and assess the company's future in comparison to regional and national competitors.

In the following chapter, we will discuss investment opportunities in private placements, limited partnerships, and thinly traded stocks.

7 Private Placements, Limited Partnerships, and Thinly Traded Stocks

Private Placements

Closely akin to investing in IPOs is getting in on private placements. The private placement can be structured in many forms, including a combination of stock and debt issues, but the securities are not available to the general public.

Private placements prove to be an effective tool for young companies to raise second- and third-stage capital to continue their growth. Reduced cost is a major reason companies embrace private placements. An initial public offering typically requires a deal at least in the $3–$5-million range with costs running in the hundreds of thousands of dollars to make economic sense. Private placements can be accomplished for much lower amounts. Private placements are a lot cheaper because they are not bound by the same rules as IPOs, which require full registration with the Securities and Exchanges Commission, a costly process. Private placements can typically be accomplished for less than half the cost of an initial public offering.

"Investors wanting to get involved in the private placements market must not only be financially qualified but must also be extremely savvy in evaluating investments," advises Warren D. Bagatelle, Managing Director of Loeb Partners Corporation in New York City.

Bagatelle stresses that private placement investors must understand the degree of risk involved. While big money can be made in the private placement market, it is not for the novice investor. For example, most private placement investments are relatively illiquid for a period of time. Likewise, the company may not go public as planned, keeping the investment tied up for an indefinite period. Finally, the deal itself may sour, resulting in a significant loss of principal for the private placement investor.

With those caveats firmly in mind, a review of a private placement illustrates the profit potential for investors astute enough to evaluate the risks and rewards of opportunities in the private placement arena.

Bagatelle interested investor Stephen Globus in the upcoming private placement involving the spinoff of Energy Research Corporation from St. Joseph Minerals in late October 1987.

"The timing was perfect. It was right after the 1987 October stock market crash and investors were skittish. It was the perfect setting for an undervaluaton of a firm with very exciting potential. There weren't a lot of investors pursuing the firm. You must have the conviction to step up to the plate when others are fleeing investments," says Globus.

Energy Research had developed a proprietary carbonate fuel cell with several advantages over conventional forms of power generation that use fossil fuels. Benefits include higher efficiency, less pollution, and greater siting flexibility.

Bagatelle, Globus, and Globus' brother drove the hour or so to Connecticut and toured the laboratory. They also met with the company president for over an hour. They came away excited by the technology and impressed with management.

"Our number one criterion in investing in private placements is the quality of management. The Energy Research management team had worked together for 15 years and had a proven track record. That eliminated the high risk associated with many startup companies. In addition, management had a financial stake in making the company a success. That's always a plus," says Globus.

Globus invested $100,000 in the company's convertible preferred stock plus the option to convert to 100,000 shares of common stock upon the occurrence of an IPO by Energy Research Corporation.

"Three years after our private placement investment, the company stock went public at $9 per share. We made $1 million each on our initial investment," says Globus.

According to Globus, other key factors in convincing them to invest in the private placement were the fact that a potential exit existed in the form of the anticipated IPO, a review of the company's five-year business plan reflected well thought-out operational and financial strategies, and other investors in the deal included investment bankers.

"I steer clear of deals proposed by accountants or lawyers. You want to make sure there is investment banker interest in the deal. They do their homework and provide an extra cushion of comfort in the economics and potential of the private placement," advises Globus.

If private placement investors opt for debt, it's wise to get an equity kicker to ensure participation in the capital gains in addition to earning interest on the debt.

Pay close attention to the five-year business plan to make sure it is well constructed. Each company objective should be backed up by specific actions designed to achieve the desired objective. The plan must also clearly spell out how the proceeds of the private placement are to be put to use.

A good rule, as Globus points out, is to make sure that the management has some "sweat equity" in the deal and that the investment banker is willing to invest in the private placement.

Keeping in touch with your local or regional investment banker or broker can keep your pulse on proposed private placement deals. Lawyers, accountants, and other consultants are also good networking contacts to keep you appraised of developing situations before it's too late. Know the track records of investment bankers. Ask for client references and make a point to call them to ascertain how well the deals performed.

Obviously, being able to see the company and its products first-hand and feeling out management and its expertise played a big role in Globus' decision to invest in Energy Research Corporation. Other factors that came into play included the economic environment in which the company would operate and an analysis of the competitive situation.

But to get into the private placement arena in the first place, you have to have the right connections. Globus' relationship with Bagatelle gave him the opportunity to learn about Energy Research Corporation's private placement. Building and maintaining close contacts with brokers, investment bankers, and other major players in the private placement market will open up doors to new opportunities to enhance your investment returns.

Aftermarket Private Placement Evaluation

As mentioned earlier, the Energy Research Corporation private placement deal worked out extremely well. The company went public in 1992 at $9 per share, generating huge profits for its investors.

How well has the firm performed since then and what are the company's future prospects? The following analysis provides food for thought and illustrates the tremendous investment gains that can be accomplished by investing in private placements.

Energy Research Corporation
3 Great Pasture Road
Danbury, CT 06813

Stock market: NASDAQ
Ticker symbol: ERCC
Telephone: 203-792-1460

Industry Review. The world market for electric power generating equipment and related services is estimated at $200 billion annually, with the United States accounting for in excess of $30 billion annually. The Administration's push for cleaner fuel sources will have a huge impact on this market and on the demand for new, more efficent, environmentally cleaner power source products.

Company Profile. Energy Research Corporation is one of the world's leading developers of advanced fuel cells for electrical power generation and has also developed significant battery technology under contracts with the U.S. government and industrial customers such as the electrical utility industry. During 1993, the company built and tested its first two full-scale, 125 KW direct fuel cells, the largest single-stack carbonate fuel cells tested worldwide.

The company has begun marketing demonstration plants and anticipates commercialization of this technology by 1998. The firm also licenses its fuel cell technology to leading manufacturing companies in the United States, Europe, and Japan such as Westinghouse, Sanyo Electric, Mitsubishi Electric, and Messerschmitt-Daimler-Benz. The license agreements provide for royalty payments as well as the right for Energy Research to use technology developed by the company's licensees in its own production.

Management Talent. Chairman Thomas L. Kempner and President and Chief Executive Officer Dr. Bernard S. Baker lead a seasoned management team in the research and development and product development fields.

Financial Status. The company possesses ample cash flow and working capital to fund research and development efforts and product marketing. Long-term debt is steadily decreasing and stands around 37 percent of total capital.

Particular Strengths. Proprietary technology and license agreements with world-class manufacturers bode well for Energy Research. Utility industry pressure to lower costs and reduce the environmental impact of power generation work in Energy Research's favor with its innovative technology. Unlike most early stage companies, Energy Research is already profitable due to revenues from strategic licensing arrangements and sales of demonstration power units.

Financial Statistics

($ millions except per-share data)

	Fiscal year ended October 31		
	1992	*1993*	*1994*
Revenues	17	22.2	30.1
Net income (loss)	0.0	.341	.220
Earnings (loss)/share	.02	.09	.06
Dividend/share	—	—	—
Long-term debt	6.6	6.2	5.8
Stock price range/share:	1992	1993	1994
High	16½	15½	13¼
Low	7⅞	8¼	9

Investment Assessment. Energy Research's backlog continues to expand with the addition of new demonstration units. The company is on the cutting edge of technology that will make utilities more cost competitive and cleaner producers of power. As the company moves toward complete commercialization of its technology in the next few years, revenues and earnings are expected to increase significantly.

The company's battery technology, although a small part of current operations, could provide a surprise kicker to future earnings possibilities. With the stock trading near the low end of its 52-week trading range of $12½ to $8½ per share and just above its offering price of $9 per share, the downside risk appears minimal. A solid long-term investment backed by a well-managed company with futuristic technology.

Limited Partnerships

From a practical standpoint, investing in many limited partnerships is similar to purchasing stock of a listed corporation. The shares of limited partnerships such as Plum Creek Timber Company, L.P. trades on the

New York Stock Exchange. Likewise, you would evaluate the prospects for these types of limited partnerships just as you would any other security purchase. What are the risks and potential rewards? How capable is management? What is their track record of successful acquisitions, turnarounds, or running day-to-day operations? How well do the company's products and/or services compete in the marketplace?

Some types of limited partnerships, such as real estate ventures and oil and gas exploration, require more specialized research and knowledge. Obviously, analyzing the income flow from rental properties and the benefits of potential tax incentives is different from looking at financial statements and analyst reports on Wal-Mart Stores, Inc. In fact, it may be wise to obtain professional advice to help you fully understand the investment parameters and risks associated with real estate, and oil and gas, and other intricate limited partnerships. The cardinal rule for investment safety is, "If you don't understand it, don't invest."

"Many investors don't realize that they have to treat income and capital gains from partnerships differently than they do for corporate common stock for federal income tax purposes. While it's not complicated, it does take some extra time and requires filing the proper partnership tax forms. If in doubt, check with your financial advisor or tax accountant," advises Russ Compton, a principal with C&S Tax Associates, Inc. in Cleveland Heights, Ohio.

The partnership will supply you with the Partnership Schedule K-1 to aid filing your income tax on partnership income distributed to you during the year. Instead of treating partnership cash distributions as totally taxable income, unit holders need to pay income tax only on their pro rata share of the partnership's taxable income, which could be lower than cash distributions. You will have to make your own calculations on any capital gains or losses from the sale of partnership units. You and your tax accountant also need to be aware that income from partnerships may not be offset by passive tax losses from other investments.

With these caveats in mind, let's review several limited partnerships.

Plum Creek Timber Company, L.P.
999 Third Avenue, Suite 2300
Seattle, WA 98104

Stock exchange: NYSE
Ticker symbol: PCL
Telephone: 206-467-3600

Industry Review. Today, the timber and wood products manufacturing businesses depend on both domestic and international economic and market forces. For example, approximately 60 percent of the timber harvested from from the Northwest Cascades Region is sold for export to Pacific Rim countries. Also, more than ever, environmental issues cloud the economic value and accessibility of specific timberlands and the costs of harvesting the timber.

Environmental interests impact new home building and general economic expansion, thus increasing or decreasing timber and wood products production. Increased competition for available timber and harvesting curtailments can significantly effect timber companies' operating costs and bottom lines.

The industry is subject to both seasonal and economic cycles. Demand for manufactured products is generally lower in the fall and winter when the construction and remodeling market activity slows, and higher in the spring and summer quarters. Domestic log sales volumes are typically at their lowest point in the second quarter during spring break-up. Export revenues are affected in part by variations in inventory levels and weather conditions.

Company Profile. Plum Creek Timber Company, L.P. is the second largest private timberland owner in the Pacific Northwest and one of the largest private timberland owners in the United States. The company has approximately 2 million acres of timberland and approximately 10.5 billion board feet of softwood timber inventory. It operates five sawmills, two plywood producing plants, a medium-density fiberboard manufacturing facility, a remanufacturing joint venture, and a chip plant.

In addition to selling harvested timber, Plum Creek manufactures and sells noncommodity products to the retail, industrial end-users, and specialty consumer markets. The partnership went public in June 1989 as a spinoff from Burlington Resources, Inc.

Management Talent. Plum Creek Timber brought over a team of seasoned industry management from Burlington Resources. President and Chief Executive Officer Richard R. Holley previously served as Vice President, Finance and Planning from October 1985 until 1993. Chairman David D. Leland previously served as President and CEO since April 1983.

Financial Status. Plum Creek Timber's current ratio is in excess of 2-to-1 and the company's cash flow is healthy. In August 1994, the partnership issued $150 million of senior unsecured notes due 2009 and bearing interest at 8.73 percent. The proceeds were used to repay a portion of the floating-rate bank debt incurred to finance the November 1993 acquisition of Montana Timberland, bringing an additional 865,000 acres of timberland into the company's timber holdings.

Particular Strengths. Extensive timber acreage and efficient plants make Plum Creek a solid play on rising timber values with worldwide economic expansion. New plants and facility enhancements in the works include:

- A $3 million automated layup line for the Columbia Falls, Montana plywood plant.
- A $2.9 million remanufacturing facility at the Evergreen, Montana sawmill location.
- A $6.7 million development project in the medium-density fiberboard facility, designed to bring a new higher-quality fiberboard product to the marketplace.

Financial Statistics

($ millions except per-unit data)

	1992	*1993*	*1994*
Revenues	440	501	579
Net income (loss)	64	91	112
Earnings (loss)/share	1.34	1.92	2.36
Distributions/unit	1.17	1.38	1.67
Long-term debt	310	544	434
Stock price range/unit:	1992	1993	1994
High	15	26¾	32½
Low	10⅞	14⅝	19⅝

Investment Assessment. Investors in Plum Creek Timber through early 1994 have earned significant gains. Since peaking at $32½ per share, the stock price has drifted to the low $20-per-share range. The price level underestimates the long-term inherent earnings and cash flow potential of the partnership's timber holdings and manufacturing capabilities.

A correction in the inventory levels, increased domestic and international demand, and newer more efficient facilities coming on stream could boost 1995 earnings to the $2.50-per-unit level or higher. At the current dividend rate, the cash dividend is more than adequately covered by projected earnings. Purchase for current income with a yield over 7 percent and for long-term capital appreciation.

Cedar Fair, L.P.
P.O. Box 5006
Sandusky, OH 44871-8006

Stock exchange: NYSE
Ticker symbol: FUN
Telephone: 419-626-0830

Industry Review. Folks in Minnesota, Ohio, and Pennsylvania could follow the stream of cars to the popular amusement parks operated by Cedar Fair, L.P. The national pattern of increasing leisure spending also bodes well for this hometown investment, as does the rebounding and vibrant economies in which the firm's amusement parks are located. Rising disposable income levels and a return to family values and outings portend better times ahead for the entertainment and leisure industry.

Company Profile. Cedar Fair, L.P. operates three seasonal amusement parks:

1. Cedar Point, along Lake Erie betweeen Cleveland and Toledo.
2. Valleyfair, near the Minneapolis/St. Paul metropolitan area.
3. Dorney Park & Wildwater Kingdom, near Allentown, Pennsylvania.

All told, the three amusement parks draw customers from a population base in excess of 65 million people. Combined, the partnership's amusement parks have been operating for a total of 252 years.

The partnership went public in 1987 at an offering price of $10 per unit. Through 1993, the partnership has distributed nearly $9 per limited partnership unit. Over the seven-year period through December 31, 1993, Cedar Fair investors have earned a compounded rate of return in excess of 24 percent.

Management Talent. President and Chief Executive Officer Richard L. Kinzel has held those positions since 1986 and been associated with Cedar Fair for over 21 years. The majority of the rest of top management claim an average of 20 years with Cedar Fair and have steered the partnership to a nearly 48 percent increase in revenues in three years.

Financial Status. During 1993, cash flow increased 24 percent and remains healthy on rising earnings.

Particular Strengths. A successful long-term track record, rising park attendance, higher in-park per capita spending, and new attractions spell higher revenues and earnings in the years ahead. For the third consecutive year, Cedar Point has been named the best amusement park in the world and, for the second straight year, its Magnum XL-200 has been voted the number 1 roller coaster on earth (as indicated by an international survey conducted by *Inside Track*).

Financial Statistics

($ millions except per-unit data)

	1992	*1993*	*1994*
Revenues	153	179	198
Net income (loss)	43	62*	63
Earnings (loss)/share	1.96	2.75*	2.79
Distributions/share	1.725	1.925	2.125
Long-term debt	50	50	50
Stock price range/unit:	1992	1993	1994
High	29⅞	36⅝	36⅝
Low	17¾	27	26¾

*Includes one-time credit for deferred taxes in the amount of $11 million or 49 cents per share.

Investment Assessment. Record attendance and earnings in 1994 and beyond should help Cedar Fair's stock price return to former heights after bouncing along to new lows in late 1994. The nearly 8 percent yield will comfort investors as they wait for the stock price to begin ratcheting steadily upward, unlike the partnership's roller coasters. Buy for fun and profits.

Cambridge Development Group
1801 Wynkoop Street
Denver, CO 80202
Telephone: 303-296-6700

When Allen Gerstenberger talks about hometown investing, he literally means a several block area from his office in downtown Denver. Gerstenberger has put his masters degree in planning from MIT and his undergraduate degree in architecture to work purchasing and renovating historic Denver buildings for a variety of uses. Gerstenberger and an associate are the two principals in Cambridge Development Group, a Colorado general partnership.

Since 1981, Cambridge Development has taken in other partners (in a project-based limited partnership arrangement), depending on specific financing requirements. Past projects include the Odd Fellows Hall and the Masonic Building, both originally constructed in 1889. Thirty limited partners joined forces with Cambridge Development Group to renovate the Odd Fellows Hall at a cost of around $6 million in 1983, while limited partners had a 60 percent interest in the $16 million restoration of the Masonic Building in 1984–1985. Both renovations won a number of local and national awards in categories such as Best Rehabilitated Commercial Project, Historical Building, Design, Historic Preservation Excellence, and Outstanding Efforts to Rebuild Historic Structure. (See Fig. 7-1.) The overall value of projects completed by Cambridge Development Group tops $100 million and encompasses approximately 1 million square feet of commercial property, 172 residential units, and 127 acres of subdivisions.

"We find prospective partners by networking people we know in the business. Our current project for Tramway Tower & Bromley Building will require $9 million to complete the historic renovation. We are looking for limited partners with $750,000 to $1 million to invest. At that level, your investors are pretty sophisticated," says Gerstenberger.

One of the attractions of undertaking major historic restoration lies in the historic investment tax credits and possible housing tax credits that may be available to limited partnership investors.

As mentioned earlier, learn the ropes before you invest or find yourself an advisor who knows the ins and outs of specific types of partnership deals. These types of opportunities are not limited to Denver; they abound across the country from major cities to small towns. To learn

Figure 7-1. The Masonic Building. *(Source: Cambridge Development Group.)*

about upcoming real estate deals, you need to travel in the right circles. Begin by asking questions. Find out who put recent deals together and asked to be notified of new projects. Then do your homework.

Thinly Traded and Neglected Stocks

One treasure trove of potential investments lies in finding local or regional stocks that are not followed closely by the investment community or the investing public at large. Because of the lack of investor knowledge, the company's stock is thinly traded and relatively minor changes in demand can create large upward price swings.

Of course, you have to perform your investigative work to determine which stocks are really underpriced by a lack of investor following and those firms whose business prospects are less than attractive, thus causing investor disinterest.

One of the benefits of purchasing these "shadow" stocks is that their market price already discounts their true value. In other words, you have downside protection against further declines and therefore a lower risk posture.

An estimated 2000-plus stocks are regularly covered by the investment research community. With over 9000 stocks traded on the listed exchanges and over-the-counter, that leaves approximately 7000 stocks without regular coverage, waiting to be discovered.

A study by Professors Avner Arbel of Cornell University and Paul Strebel of the State University of New York, as reported in the *Journal of Portfolio Management*, showed analyst-neglected portfolios (0–1 analysts) earning an average return of 16.4 percent in the 1970–1979 period, compared to a 12.7 percent return for moderately followed (2–3 analysts) stocks and only a 9.4 percent return for highly followed (4 or more analysts) stocks.

The American Association of Individual Investors publishes an annual listing of shadow stocks that are out of the glare of research analysts and institutional investors. Criteria for making the list include:

- Common stock outstanding with a market value between $20 million and $100 million.
- Relatively low institutional ownership (no more than 15 percent).
- Positive earnings per share for the most recent two years and five years of financial data available.
- Companies not in the financial industry (bank, investment broker, etc).

For 1994, 293 stocks passed the screening criteria, 74 more than in 1993. Throughout the year, The *AAII Journal* uses its shadow stock list to illustrate how individuals can analyze the prospects of specific stocks by applying a variety of secondary screens and to demonstrate how these techniques might be useful. See Table 7-1 for a portion of AAII's shadow stock listing. (AAII can be contacted at 625 North Michigan Avenue, Chicago, IL 60611-3110, 312-280-0170.)

As you can see, there's every type of company imaginable, from A to Z. Business service firms account for the largest single sector of companies appearing on the shadow list with 8.1 percent, followed by business data processing (7.75 percent), health firms (7.4 percent), utilities-gas-other (6.7 percent), and electronics (6.0 percent). With the exception of utilities, the other industries with a high concentration of shadow firms might be ripe for seeking out potential takeover candidates as their industries consolidate.

Other sources for uncovering shadow stocks include *Moody's Industrial Manual, Moody's OTC Industrial Manual, NASDAQ Fact Book and Company Directory, Standard & Poor's Stock Guide, Standard & Poor's Stock Reports,* and *Standard & Poor's Register of Corporations, Directors, and Executives. Nelson's Directory of Investment Research* lists the analysts that cover each firm.

Preferred stocks represent another form of thinly traded stocks that the astute investor can capitalize on. There are more than 400 preferred issues trading on the New York Stock Exchange alone, as well as several mutual funds specializing in preferred stocks.

Investors like preferred stock because it provides a protected stream of income plus more safety of principal than offered by common stock. Preferreds are hybrid securities, a cross between common stocks and bonds. They provide equity ownership in the company with some voting powers, but, since they pay a stated rate of return in the form of a fixed dividend, they also resemble bonds. Preferred shareholders must receive their dividends before any dividends are paid on the common stock.

In addition to the dividend preferential treatment, preferred stock also possesses a higher ranking in the ownership status of the company. In the event of the company's liquidation or bankruptcy, preferred stockholders have a prior claim to company assets over common stockholders but behind that of bondholders.

For the most part, preferred stock market prices respond more to changes in market interest rates than to the stock market in general or to the market price of the company's common stock. Since the preferred dividend rate and thus its yield is fixed, once the preferred stock is purchased, investors must compare its yield with competing investment alternatives in terms of both yield and safety.

Table 7-1. AAII Shadow Stocks—Partial Listing

Company	*Ticker symbol*	*Industry*
Acmat Corporation	ACMT	Business services
Adams Research & Energy	AE	Oil refining, marketing
Advance Ross	AROS	Heavy machinery
AEP Industries	AEPI	Rubber-plastic
Airlease Ltd.	FLY	Airlines
American Enterprises	ACES	Recreation
American Filtrona	AFIL	Rubber-plastic
American Fructose B	AFCB	Foods-packaged goods
Analysis & Technology	AATI	Business services
Arch Petroleum	ARCH	Oil, natural gas services
ARX, Inc.	ARX	Aerospace
Aztec Manufacturing	AZTC	Machinery—heavy
Bangor-Hydro-Electric	BGR	Electric utilities
Bay Meadows	CJ	Recreation
Big O Tires	BIGO	Rubber-plastic
Boston Acoustics	BOSA	Electronics
Cache Inc.	CACH	Retail apparel
Cagle's Inc. A	CGLA	Foods-meats-dairy
Cavco Industries, Inc.	CVCO	Building
CIS Technologies	CISI	Business data processing
COMCOA	CCOA	Communications
Concord Fabrics	CIS	Textile manufacturing
DAKA International	DKAI	Hotels-motels-resorts
Datakey, Inc.	DKEY	Precision instruments
Dickenson Mines A	DMLA	Precious metals
Drew Industries	DREW	Multi-industry
Ecology/Environment A	EEI	Electrical equipment
Filtertek, Inc.	FTK	Automotive
Fonar Corporation	FONR	Health
G-III Apparel Group Ltd.	GIII	Shoes—leather
Hako Minuteman	HAKO	Housewares—furnishings
Hycor Biomedical	HYBO	Drug manufacturers
Interpoint Corporation	INTP	Electronics
Jean Philippe Fragrances	JEAN	Cosmetic—personal
Kleinert's, Inc.	KLRT	Retail—apparel
Knape & Vogt Mfg.	KNAP	Building
LESCO, Inc.	LSCO	Chemicals
Mauna Loa	NUT	Food production
Norex America	NXA	Freight-shipping
Odetics, Inc. A	OA	Electronics
Parlux	PARL	Cosmetic—personal
Plasti-Line	SIGN	Business equipment
Quiksilver, Inc.	QUIK	Textiles—apparel
Reflectone, Inc.	RFTN	Aerospace
Scientific Technologies	STIZ	Precision instruments
SJW Corp.	SJW	Utilities-gas-other

Table 7-1. AAII Shadow Stocks—Partial Listing (Continued)

Company	*Ticker symbol*	*Industry*
Total-Tel USA	TELU	Communications
Tuscarora Plastics	TUSC	Paper-packaging
Uranium Resources	URIX	Metals-nonferrous-coal
Virco Manufacturing	VIR	Business equipment
Waverly, Inc.	WAVR	Publishing
Xscribe Corporation	XSCR	Business equipment
Zoom Telephonics Inc.	ZOOMF	Communications
ZYGO Corporation	ZIGO	Health

SOURCE: American Association of Individual Investors.

The main appeal of preferred stock lies in its ability to deliver a generous yield compared to other investment alternatives combined with a higher degree of principal safety. Another of the preferred stock's appeals is that so few people understand it. Imperfect investor knowledge creates an inefficient market and unique investment opportunities. Therefore, with a little research, overall returns can be boosted with a selective investment in preferreds.

Adjustable rate provisions protect the investor against a decrease in the preferred stock market price, since they allow the investor to earn a higher yield as interest rates rise.

There's another way for preferred stockholders to share in higher dividends. The participating preferred stock receives a specified dividend but also has the right to share in any excess earnings that would normally be distributed to the common stock shareholders.

Some preferred stock issues contain a cumulative clause permitting dividends to accumulate if dividend payouts are suspended by the board of directors. These accumulated dividends will first have to be paid out to preferred shareholders before any dividends can be paid on the common stock.

The convertible preferred carries a provision allowing shareholders to convert their holdings into a certain number of common shares of the company at a specified price. The convertible preferred offers the best of both worlds. It provides an attractive yield combined with the added bonus of allowing the investor to participate in the upside move of the underlying common stock through its convertibility feature.

When deciding to purchase a preferred stock, take into consideration a number of critical factors. First, take a hard look at the underlying credit of the issuing company. Investigate how both the shares and debt issues are rated. What has been the company's long-term credit track record? Are there problems looming on the industry's or company's horizon that could impact the firm's ability to pay dividends as scheduled?

Pay attention to the call provisions. Typically, most preferreds are noncallable for five years, protecting the investor for that length of time or for the remaining period of time before the initial call date if market interest rates decline.

Use the research department of mutual funds that specialize in preferred stocks to help uncover thinly traded preferred stocks in your neck of the woods. For example, a perusal of the portfolio holdings of the Vanguard Preferred Stock Fund (800-662-7447) reflects hometown investment options in a variety of industries from every part of the country. Florida investors could take a stake in the Florida Power & Light 6.75 percent preferred, while Delaware residents could play the chemical industry with the $4.50 preferred of E. I. du Pont De Nemours & Company. In Illinois, Household International, Inc. 7.355 preferreds represent the consumer products market. On the West Coast, California investors could invest in the insurance industry via Transamerica Corporation 8.5 percent preferreds or in the banking industry with Bank America Corporation 7.875 percent preferreds.

Ask your broker about thinly traded preferreds and other securities of quality companies in your region of the country. Scour the listings of local and regional companies. Then track the stock prices and trading volume of the companies that your investment analysis has led you to believe are undervalued in the market. Take your position in these quality companies early, and wait for the market to recognize their true value and drive their stock prices upward.

The ESOP Advantage

You can own a piece of Hometown, America right where you work. Shares owned by employee stock ownership plans (ESOPs) can be an important way for you to own stock in the company you know best, the one you work for. Over 10 million Americans own a part of the company they work for through approximately 9500 employee stock ownership plans. According to the National Center for Employee Ownership in Oakland, California, employee ownership has been growing at 300 to 600 new plans per year, with 300,000 to 600,000 new plan participants a year in recent years. ESOPs control close to $60 billion in corporate stock with employees owning another $90 billion in company stock through a variety of other programs including stock purchase, profit sharing, and 401(k) plans.

Examples of large companies with large employee ownership are Avis, W.L. Gore Associates (maker of Gore-Tex), Publix Supermarkets, Quad/Graphics (major U.S. printer), and UAL Corporation (United Airlines). You may say, "Fine, but I don't work for Avis or United Airlines." The fact is that 85 percent of ESOPs are in private companies and an estimated nearly 15 percent of the United States work force are employee-owners. Figure 7-2 shows the dramatic increase in employee owners over the ten-year period 1983–1993.

Therefore, your chance to invest in an ESOP increases with each passing year. Companies establish ESOPs for a variety of reasons. For example, it's one way for an owner to retire without having to close or sell off the business to another company. ESOPs also deliver a way to borrow at a lower after-tax cost due to its unique structure and ability for the company to repay ESOP loans with principal and interest that are both deductible. Finally, many companies establish ESOPs as an added employee benefit to attract and retain the best employees.

"You don't just invest in a company through its ESOP just because you work there. Make sure it is a good investment in relation to other investment alternatives," advises Corey Rosen, Executive Director for the National Center for Employee Ownership.

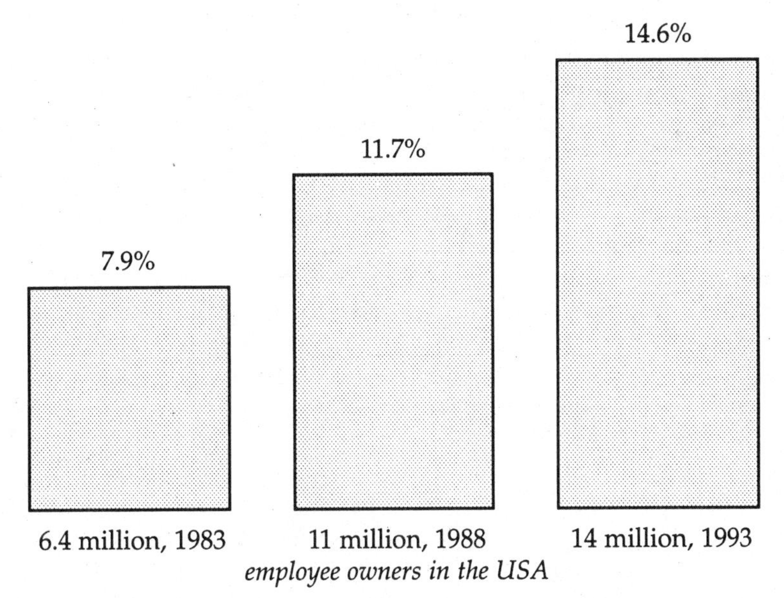

Figure 7-2. Increase of employee owners of total U.S. work force, estimate. (SOURCE: National Center for Employee Ownership, Oakland, CA, 510-272-9461.)

That is sound advice, especially since you already have a substantial investment in your employer—your regular income and possible retirement plans.

The Stone Equipment Construction Experience

Tucked away in Honeoye, New York, Stone Construction Equipment, Inc. competes in the tough international construction equipment market. Back in 1986, company heir Alan Stone no longer wanted to run the then 20-year-old company. An ESOP, which already owned 30 percent of the company in 1979, increased its ownership to 100 percent by 1986.

Since then, annual revenues have surged nearly threefold to $35 million from $12 million. On top of that, employee owners have squeezed out the following operating efficiencies:

- Switching to just-in-time inventory slashed scrap costs by $150,000.
- Employees reduced setup time on a mixer line by 50–90 percent.
- Cycle time on the mixer line was cut from 10 days to 2 days.
- Material handling decreased from 22 employees to 2 people.
- Work in process was reduced by 75 percent.
- Finished goods inventory was reduced by 50 percent.
- Overall productivity increased by 35 to 40 percent.

As testimony to the progress made by Stone Construction Equipment, *Industry Week* magazine selected Stone as one of America's best manufacturing plants in 1991. All of this works to make the company more profitable and the employees' shares more valuable.

Since 1991, the value of Stone Construction Equipment's stock has grown at an annual rate of 16 percent. Not a bad return by anybody's criterion.

Moving from private placements, limited partnerships, and thinly traded stocks, we will look at hometown investing through the regional mutual fund approach in the next chapter.

8
Taking the Regional Mutual Fund Approach

Regional Mutual Funds

A number of regional mutual funds can fit your hometown investment strategies and goals. In addition, they are a great place to mine for treasure in the form of interesting investment alternatives with a hometown flavor. By sifting through the portfolio holdings of regional mutual funds, you can discover attractive companies poised to perform well in the future.

There are a number of regional mutual funds across the nation from which to construct your portfolio. Let the mutual fund investment managers and advisors conduct your up-front analysis work and develop a prospective list of investments for you. Then, you can perform additional analysis on your own to narrow down the list to the specific securities that best fit your investment goals and risk parameters.

A review of regional mutual fund holdings clearly illustrates the breadth of investment opportunities available within a single region of the country. There's something for every type of investor. Companies held in regional mutual fund portfolios run the gamut from local and regional banks to utilities, and from industrial businesses such as automotive and timber to service industries such as nonbanking financial services to transportation companies.

A list of the available regional funds appears at the end of this chapter. We will analyze a number of regional funds for investment consideration, and take a look at some of their more promising holdings for individual purchase for your own account. In addition, close analysis of regional mutual fund holdings and changes in those holdings can help the alert investor decipher "hot" industries and investment trends.

IAI Regional Fund
P.O. Box 357
Minneapolis, MN 55440
Telephone: 800-945-3863
Ticker symbol: IARGX
Investment advisor: Investment Advisors, Inc.

Year begun: 1980
Assets: $596 million
Minimum investment: $5000
Load: None
Annual expense ratio: 1.25 percent
Turnover: 163 percent

Investment Strategy. The IAI Regional Fund invests in the dynamic economic environment of the upper Midwest. It searches out reasonably priced companies possessing outstanding growth potential. Its target region includes its headquarters base of Minnesota plus Illinois, Iowa, Montana, Nebraska, North Dakota, South Dakota, and Wisconsin. Most of the companies that IAI Regional Fund invests in are located within one day's drive of the mutual fund's headquarters, making it easy to keep in close contact with investments and promising new opportunities within the region. To date, the fund has traditionally outperformed the S&P 500.

Returns

One-year	.68 percent through 12/31/94
Five-year	8.92 percent through 12/31/94
Ten-year	15.83 percent through 12/31/94

Representative Major Holdings (9/30/94)

Company	*Industry*	*HQ*
Motorola	Technology	Illinois
McDonald's	Fast Food	Illinois
SciMed Life Systems	Medical Products	Minnesota
Glendale Federal Bank	Finance	California
Automotive Industries	Industrial	Minnesota
ADC Telecommunications	Telecommunications	Minnesota
MGIC Investment	Finance	Wisconsin
NWNL	Insurance	Minnesota
Snap-On Tools	Industrial	Wisconsin
Casey's General Store	Food-retail	Iowa

Portfolio Composition. The top five industry sectors of the IAI Regional Fund consisted of consumer cyclicals (17.0 percent), industrial (15.2 percent), financial/insurance (11.0 percent), consumer noncyclicals (10.6 percent), and technology (8.1 percent). The fund maintains a heavy concentration of consumer cyclicals poised to benefit from continued economic expansion.

Recent Top Performers. Examples of big winners for the annual report year ended March 31, 1994 included:

- Best Buy, a Minneapolis-headquartered consumer electronics discount retailer (+44 percent).
- Andrew Corporation, an Orland Park, Illinois electronic communications products supplier (+38 percent).
- ADC Telecommunications, a Bloomington, Minnesota telecommunications firm providing switching gear to large telephone, cable television, and cellular operators (+32 percent).

Portfolio Holding Evaluations. IAI Regional Fund held:

- 175,000 shares of Banta Corporation for a stake in the publishing industry.
- 735,000 shares of retailer Casey's General Stores (a nearly 30 percent increase over the prior quarter).
- 312,000 shares of MGIC Investment Corporation (a more than tripling of prior holdings) in the financial services sector.

Banta Corporation
2235 Main Street
P.O. Box 8003
Menasha, WI 54952-8003

Stock exchange: NASDAQ
Ticker symbol: BNTA
Telephone: 414-751-7777

Industry Review. Banta Corporation operates in the specialty printing and graphics services industry, which is enjoying cyclical growth. Acquisition consolidation of the highly fragmented industry is also providing growth opportunities in strategic markets. Likewise, firms with the financial strength to invest in state-of-the-art printing technology will be at the forefront of the industry in terms of revenue and earnings growth potential.

Company Profile. Banta Corporation ranks as one of North America's leading providers of printing and graphic services and as a Fortune 500 company. The firm serves publishers of educational and general books, special-interest magazines, consumer and business catalogs, and direct marketing materials.

Banta has been hot on the acquisition trail to expand revenues and market share. It purchased Danbury Printing & Litho, Inc. in Connecticut during March 1994 and completed the acquisition of Kent, WA-based United Graphics, Inc. during the third quarter of 1994.

Management Talent. Chairman and Chief Executive Officer Calvin W. Aurand, Jr. heads a seasoned management team with extensive experience both at Banta and other industry firms. The company recently beefed up its management team with the addition of Donald D. Belcher as President and Chief Operating Officer. Belcher came to Banta after serving as Senior Group Vice President of Avery Dennison Corporation, a diversified manufacturer of office products.

Financial Status. Strong revenues and earnings growth boosted cash flow per share from under $3 per share in 1991 to the $4-per-share level in 1994. In the same vein, Banta's working capital stands around $100 million. Long-term debt rose from less than $50 million in 1993 to over $70 million with the two acquisitions. Look for long-term debt to steadily decrease with the exception of capital needed for any additional company purchases.

Particular Strengths. Banta's financial prowess will allow it to take advantage of strategic acquisitions as they present themselves. In addition, sufficient capital resources help the company stay abreast of the latest printing technology. The company is also moving strongly into related businesses such as computer software documentation, point-of-purchase materials, packaging, and direct marketing materials.

Financial Statistics

($ millions except per-share data)

	1992	*1993*	*1994*
Revenues	637	691	811
Net income (loss)	36	41	47
Earnings (loss)/share	1.79	2.03	2.33
Dividend/share	.41	.47	.53
Long-term debt	52	46	70
Stock price range/share:	1992	1993	1994
High	27⅞	37	38½
Low	16½	26⅝	27

Investment Assessment. Despite strong revenue and earnings performance, Banta's stock price has drifted steadily downward since peaking at $38½ per share in March 1994, hitting a low of $27 per share in late November 1994. The company's underlying fundamentals and a rebounding economy spell more progress ahead. The stock is undervalued, especially when you factor in recent acquisitions and other operation expansions such as new presses and the new Digital Services operation on the West Coast. Buy for long-term capital appreciation.

Casey's General Stores, Inc.

See the discussion in Chap. 9.

MGIC Investment Corporation
MGIC Plaza
P.O. Box 488
Milwaukee, WI 53202

Stock exchange: NYSE
Ticker symbol: MTG
Telephone: 414-347-6812

Industry Review. MGIC Investment Corporation operates in the mortgage insurance industry. Rising interest rates have put a damper on mortgages and mortgage refinancings. This could be offset by the expanding demand for homes from first-time buyers, if higher interest rates don't scare them off altogether.

Company Profile. MGIC Investment Corporation provides mortgage insurance to lenders to protect against loss from defaults on low down payment residential mortgage loans. It also provides other mortgage and real estate services and consulting.

Management Talent. President and Chief Executive Officer William H. Lacy took over the company reins in 1985 and maneuvered the company from the brink of disaster to a successful turnaround. He is also past president of the Mortgage Insurance Companies of America and serves on a number of committees of the Mortgage Bankers Association, National Association of Home Builders Mortgage Roundtable, and the Lender's Service, Inc. Advisory Board.

Financial Status. Both Moody's Investors Service and Standard & Poor's raised the insurance firm's financial strength rating of MGIC during August and October 1994, respectively. The upgrading reflects the company's conservative underwriting standards, favorable claims experience, strong market position, diversified insured portfolio, and adequate capital. The new ratings are Aa2 (Moody's) and AA+ (S&P).

Particular Strengths. Strong bookings promise to keep revenues and earnings on a roll. The company has little long-term debt and can support growth with internal funds. Conservative underwriting standards and a high-quality investment portfolio should keep losses to a minimum.

Financial Statistics

($ millions except per-share data)

	1992	*1993*	*1994*
Revenues	322	404	502
Net income (loss)	102	127	159
Earnings (loss)/share	1.74	2.16	2.70
Dividends/share	.14	.145	.16
Long-term debt	37	37	36
Stock price range/share:	1992	1993	1994
High	25¾	35¾	34¼
Low	15¾	24¾	25

Investment Assessment. Investor concern over the impact of rising interest rates on MGIC's future mortgage insurance business kept the firm's stock price in the middle of its 52-week trading range for most of 1994. However, MGIC's ability to post significantly higher earnings over previous year results pushed the stock price to new highs in early 1995. The worst is over as far as interest rate hikes are concerned. Besides, they don't impact mortgage insurer MGIC as dramatically as they do mortgage lenders. Look for the higher earnings trend to continue.

Paine Webber Regional Financial Growth Fund, Inc.
1285 Ave. of the Americas, 10th floor
New York, NY 10019
Telephone: 800-647-1568
Ticker symbol: PREAX
Investment advisor: Mitchell Hutchens Asset Management Inc.

Year begun: 1986
Assets: $64 million
Minimum investment: $1000
Load: 4.5 percent maximum
Annual expense ratio: 1.44 percent
Turnover: 22 percent

Investment Strategy. Paine Webber Regional Financial Growth Fund invests in financial institutions in various regions across the country, shifting the portfolio mix based on changing economic conditions within the different regions. The fund seeks long-term capital appreciation by investing at least 65 percent of its assets in undervalued equity securities of regional banks, thrift institutions, financial holding companies, and insurance companies. The fund's performance improved dramatically after it ended its closed-end fund status in April 1990.

Returns

One-year:	–.075	percent through 12/31/94
Three-year:	14.92	percent through 12/31/94
Five year:	17.09	percent through 12/31/94

Representative Major Holdings

Company	*Industry*	*HQ*
Citicorp	Money center	New York
First Empire State	Regional banking	New York
BayBanks, Inc.	Regional banking	Massachusetts
Federal National Mortgage Association	Financial services	Washington, DC
Republic New York Corp	Money center	New York
First National Bank/Anchorage	Regional banking	Alaska
Northern Trust Corp.	Regional banking	Illinois
KeyCorp	Regional banking	Ohio
Heritage Financial Services	Regional banking	Illinois
Mercantile	Regional banking	Missouri

Portfolio Composition. Paine Webber Regional Financial Growth Fund has been shifting portfolio holdings away from money center banks and insurance companies which have already posted large earnings improvements. The fund is fairly well distributed across the country with Eastern regional and Midwestern regional banks accounting for the largest shares of 25 and 22 percent, respectively. Other major sectors include Western regional banks and Southern regional banks with 13 percent of portfolio assets each.

Recent Top Performers. The fund cashed in its gains on two personal lines insurers: The Progressive Corporation in Mayfield Heights, Ohio and Allied Group, Inc. of Des Moines, Iowa.

Portfolio Holding Evaluation. Paine Webber Regional Financial Growth Fund held 30,000 shares of Zions Bancorporation worth some $1.1 million.

Zions Bancorporation
1380 Kennecott Building
Salt Lake City, UT 84133

Stock exchange: NASDAQ
Ticker symbol: ZION
Telephone: 801-524-4787

Industry Review. Zions Bancorporation serves a vibrant three-state intermountain market area (Utah, Arizona, and Nevada), which continues to outpace the nation in key economic statistics such as new job growth, low unemployment, and business startups. The intermountain region is benefiting from increased mining activity, rising tourism, increased consumer demand, and an influx of people and companies leaving states such as California.

Company Profile. Zions Bancorporation is a $5.5 billion bank-holding company with over 100 offices in the three-state region. Banking subsidiaries operate under the names Zions First National Bank, Nevada State Bank, and Zions National Bank of Arizona. The company also provides related financial services such as mortgages, insurance, and brokerage. The company serves the financing and banking needs of corporate and retail businesses in its service area.

In August 1993, Zions acquired Discount Corporation of New York, a primary dealer in U.S. government securities. The move expanded and strengthened Zions' position as the premier institutional investment sales firm in the Intermountain West and one of only two primary dealers of government securities headquartered in the Western United States.

Management Talent. Roy W. Simmons and Harris H. Simmons head Zions Bancorporation as Chairman and President and CEO, respectively. They have successfully guided the bank holding company to a string of record years of net income.

Financial Status. For the 12-month period ended September 30, 1994, total assets increased 25 percent to $5.5 billion while interest income increased some 20 percent. Equally important, nonperforming assets continue to steadily decrease from 1.29 percent at the end of the third quarter in 1993 to .79 percent as of September 30, 1994. Return on average common equity came in at an impressive 18.7 percent for the first three quarters of 1994.

Particular Strengths. Zions has a strong banking franchise in an economically healthy market area. The bank's asset quality also remains high. Zions is Utah's largest mortgage lender. Although the company has turned in strong earnings performances, management is not sitting on its laurels. The company hired KPMG Peat Marwick and First Manhattan Consulting Group during the third quarter of 1994 to review the company's cost structure and asset/liability management and reporting systems to eke out even better operating efficiencies.

Financial Statistics. These are restated to reflect the acquisition of National Bancorp of Arizona.

($ millions except per-share data)

	1993	*1994*	
Net interest income	175	199	
Net income (loss)	58	64	
Earnings (loss)/share	4.08*	4.37	
Dividends/share	.98	1.16	
Stock price range/share:	1992	1993	1994
High	39	49¼	42
Low	19¾	36	33½

*Excluding effects of accounting change totaling $1.7 million or 12 cents per share.

Investment Assessment. The bank's upper trading range has finally broken through the $40-per-share level, after virtually treading water for months as indicated on Fig. 8-1. Look for higher earnings and stock prices.

Paragon Gulf South Growth Fund
4900 Sears Tower
Chicago, IL 60606
Telephone: 800-525-7907
Ticker symbol: PGSGX
Investment advisor: Premier Investment Advisors

Year begun: 1989
Assets: $82 million
Load: 4.5 percent maximum
Minimum investment: $250
Annual expense ratio: .97 percent
Turnover: 24 percent

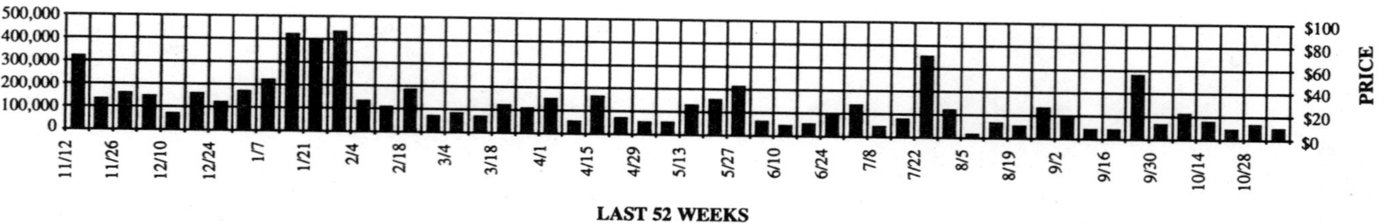

Figure 8-1. Zions Bancorporation trading history. (SOURCE: The Red Chip Review™ © *Crown Point Publishing, Inc., 1994, P.O. Box 40028, Portland, OR 97240. Phone: (503) 241-1265. Fax: (503) 241-5067. Information is obtained from sources believed to be reliable, but its accuracy and completeness are not guaranteed.*)

Investment Strategy. Despite being headquartered in Chicago under the Paragon Portfolio umbrella, Paragon Gulf South Growth Fund portfolio selection and management takes place in Baton Rouge, Louisiana. The fund seeks growth through investment in strategic Gulf South industries and companies positioned to perform well.

Returns

One-year:	–11.86 percent through 12/31/94
From inception:	12.14 percent average annual through 12/31/94

Representative Major Holdings

Company	*Industry*	*HQ*
Input/Output, Inc.	Energy	Texas
Coventry Corporation	Consumer noncyclical	Tennessee
Office Depot, Inc.	Office supplies	Florida
Nucor Corporation	Steel	North Carolina
LDDS WorldCom	Telecommunications	Georgia
Atlantic Southeast Air	Transportation	Georgia
Leader Financial Corp.	Finance	Ohio
First Financial Management Corp.	Finance	Georgia
Medaphis Corporation	Finance	Georgia
Coral Gables Federal	Finance	Florida

Portfolio Composition. Paragon Gulf South Growth Fund maintains approximately 90 percent of its total assets in the common stock of companies within the Gulf region running from North Carolina south to Florida and west to Texas. Consumer cyclical and finance companies comprise the two largest investment sectors, with approximately 27 and 24 percent of portfolio assets, respectively. Other major sectors include energy (nearly 12 percent), basic materials/natural resources (7 percent), consumer noncyclical (almost 7 percent), technology (5 percent), and transportation (4 percent). The balance of the portfolio consists of corporate debt and repurchase agreements.

Recent Top Performers. Regional thrifts such as Coral Gables Federal, Great Financial Corporation, and Gwinnett Bancshares turned in good performances in 1994, as did oil service companies (Input-Output and Landmark Graphics), steel (Nucor), and technology (Dallas Semiconductor).

Portfolio Holding Evaluation. Paragon Gulf South Growth Fund held positions in:

- Ethyl Corporation spinoff Albemarle Corporation (45,200 shares worth $728,000).
- Rapidly expanding Gwinnett Bancshares, Inc. (50,000 shares worth nearly $1.2 million).
- Aggressive telecommunications giant LDDS Communication, Inc. (180,000 shares valued at $3.3 million).

Albemarle Corporation
330 South Fourth Street
P.O. Box 1335
Richmond, VA 23210

Stock exchange: NYSE
Ticker symbol: ALB
Telephone: 804-788-6000

Industry Review. Albemarle Corporation operates within the specialty chemical industry providing a wide range of products to a variety of manufacturers of agricultural, detergent, electronic, glass, personal care, petroleum, pharmaceutical, photographic, and polymer products. Although the specialty chemicals industry is extremely competitive, Albemarle's broad product line and customer base gives the firm a competitive edge.

Company Profile. Albemarle Corporation was spun off from Ethyl Corporation in February 1994. Although the company's headquarters is based in Richmond, Virginia, the firm's executive offices are located in Baton Rouge, Louisiana and the company maintains worldwide office, plant, and terminal facilities. Overseas operations contribute approximately 40 percent of annual revenues. (See the discussion of spinoffs in Chap. 4.)

Albemarle is the world's largest supplier of alpha olefins, the world's second largest producer of bromine chemicals, and North America's largest producer of ibuprofen. The company's products go into the manufacture of literally hundreds of household and industrial products such as bleaches, disinfectants, over-the-counter drugs, building materials, office equipment, oil exploration compounds, packaging, pesticides, and semiconductors.

Management Talent. Chairman and Chief Executive Officer Floyd D. Gottwald, Jr. and President and Chief Operating Officer E. Gary Cook head a management team with vast industry experience with Ethyl and other companies such as E. I. duPont de Nemours and Company.

Financial Status. Albemarle Corporation sports in excess of $200 million in working capital, sufficient to cover projected operations and growth. The spinoff from Ethyl included some $382 million in long-term debt on a pro forma basis. At the end of the third quarter on September 30, 1994, long-term debt stood at $256 million.

Particular Strengths. In spite of intense pricing pressure and disruptions in the ethylene supply chain, the company increased both revenues and earnings over 1993 levels while it was still operating as a subsidiary of Ethyl Corporation. Albemarle's international presence should contribute to strong revenue and earnings growth as the international economic environment improves and the firm turns the international profitability picture around.

Financial Statistics

($ millions except per-share data)

	*1993**	*1994*
Revenues	903	1081
Net income (loss)	22	51
Earnings (loss)/share	.27	.79
Dividends/share	NM	.20
Long-term debt	95	252
Stock price range/share:		1994
High		17⅝
Low		12½

*Pro forma historical as subsidiary of Ethyl Corporation.
NM = Not meaningful

Investment Assessment. Albemarle trades at a price/earnings ratio (based on projected 1994 and 1995 earnings) below that of other chemical industry firms. As the company delivers consistent performance, this differential should be corrected with a resulting rise in Albemarle's stock price. Purchase for long-term capital appreciation as the domestic and international economies rebound.

Gwinnett Bancshares, Inc.
750 Perry Street
Lawrenceville, GA 30245

Stock exchange: NASDAQ
Ticker symbol: GBSI
Telephone: 404-995-6000

Gwinnett Bancshares, Inc. provided retail and commercial banking services to Gwinnett County, one of metropolitan Atlanta's fastest growing areas. In late 1994, Gwinnett shareholders voted to merge its operations with and be a part of Bank South Corporation headquartered in Atlanta (NASDAQ: BKSO).

LDDS WorldCom
515 East Amite Street
Jackson, MS 39201

Stock exchange: NASDAQ
Ticker symbol: WCOM
Telephone: 601-360-8600

Industry Review. The telecommunications industry has experienced unprecedented technological change in the past decade and the pace is accelerating. At the same time, changes in the regulatory environment have dramatically altered the competitive forces that shape the industry.

Digital transmission and fiber optics capabilities have greatly enhanced the quality and range of telecommunications products and services available to customers.

Company Profile. LDDS WorldCom provides long-distance services to the entire United States and many foreign countries. In a move designed to expand its international capabilities, LDDS acquired IDB Communication Group, Inc. in 1994. On another front, LDDS inked a $2.5 billion agreement to acquire WilTel Network Services from The Williams' Companies.

The WilTel acquisition will boost LDDS revenues to the $3-billion-per-year mark and make the company a strong competitor of the nation's three largest long-distance carriers—AT&T Corporation, MCI Communications Corporation, and Sprint Corporation. It would also deliver some 11,000 miles of state-of-the-art digital network system into the LDDS fold, along with access to another 40,000 miles through a WilTel joint venture agreement.

Management Talent. President and Chief Executive Officer Bernard J. Ebbers has served in those capacities since 1985 and engineered the rise of the company from a bit player to a major force in the telecommunications industry. The Board of Directors also brings significant industry expertise to the table. Chairman John W. Kluge also serves as Chairman and President of Metromedia Company (Metromedia owns over 20 percent of LDDS outstanding shares of common stock).

Financial Status. LDDS had already arranged financing for the WilTel acquisition, which received Federal Trade Commission approval under the Hart-Scott-Rodino Act. The acquisition promises to deliver significant operating synergies once fully merged into LDDS during 1995.

Particular Strengths. Strong internal growth coupled with major acquisitions help round out LDDS' communications network and garner additional market share. Innovative products such as prepaid long-distance cards and frame relay systems keep internal growth humming, as does successful marketing of widely ranging telecommunications agreements with major corporate firms such as Avis Rent-A-Car Systems, Inc. and Fairchild Communications Services Company.

Financial Statistics

($ millions except per-share data)

	1992	*1993*	*9 months 1993*	*9 months 1994*
Revenues	801	1145	752	1276
Net income (loss)	(6)*	104	63	98
Earnings (loss)/share	(.09)*	.85	.62	.76
Dividends/share	—	—	—	—
Long-term debt	334	526	526	519
Stock price range/share:	1992	1993	1994	
High	15⅛	26⅜	29½	
Low	8⅜	14¼	14	

*Includes extraordinary loss of $5.8 million or 6 cents per share.

Investment Assessment. Since hitting a high of $29½ per share in early 1994, LDDS' stock price has drifted to the middle $20-per-share range. Investor concern over the level of debt taken on to finance the WilTel acquisition may account for the drop in the company's stock price. The concerns are overblown. LDDS' management will squeeze out plentiful synergies to improve operations and the firm's bottom line. Purchase for long-term appreciation and a solid bet on the surging telecommunications industry.

The Roulston Midwest Growth Fund
4000 Chester Avenue
Cleveland, OH 44103
Telephone: 800-332-6459
Ticker symbol: RMGRX
Investment advisor: Roulston & Company

Year begun: 1993
Assets: $30 million
Load: None
Minimum investment: $5000
Annual expense ratio: 1.5 percent
Turnover: Not meaningful

Investment Strategy. The Roulston Midwest Growth Fund targets long-term capital appreciation by investing at least 65 percent of its portfolio assets in companies headquartered or maintaining a substantial operating presence in states bordering the Great Lakes such as Illinois, Indiana, Michigan, Minnesota, Ohio, Pennsylvania, Western New York, and Wisconsin. Although the fund is a newcomer, investment advisor Roulston & Company has been tracking the fortunes of Midwest companies since the midsixties. Management stresses a stock picking focus within the geographical regions it follows.

Returns

One-year:	7.22 percent through 12-31-94
Since inception	13.94 percent annualized 12-31-94

Representative Major Holdings

Company	*Industry*	*HQ*
Perry Drug Stores	Drug store	Michigan
Invacare Corporation	Hospital equipment	Ohio
Rite Aid Corporation	Discount drug	Pennsylvania
Ball Corporation	Containers	Indiana
Consolidated Stores Corp.	Retail	Ohio
RB&W Corporation	Fasteners	Ohio
Telxon Corporation	Microcomputers	Ohio
Bearings Incorporated	Bearings	Ohio
Duriron Company, Inc.	Control equipment	Ohio
Star Banc Corporation	Banking	Ohio

Portfolio Composition. The fund's portfolio has included some of the Great Lakes region's old-line major industrial companies such as Cincinnati Milicron, Inc. and Cooper Tire & Rubber Company, as well as relatively newcomers to the scene like start-up company Invacare Corporation and spinoff Geon.

Recent Top Performers. Companies that have performed well in the Roulston Midwest Growth Fund include Lamson & Sessions Company (construction products), Pioneer-Standard Electronics, Inc. (industrial electronics), and Geon (plastics).

Portfolio Holding Evaluation

Cooper Tire & Rubber Company
P.O. Box 550
Findlay, OH 45839-0550

Stock exchange: NYSE
Ticker symbol: CTB
Telephone: 419-423-1321

Industry Review. Rising automotive production, rising miles driven, and high average age of cars on the road (now approximately 8 years) all point to increased tire production to meet demand.

Company Profile. Cooper Tire & Rubber Company rates as a growing player in the global tire market. Ranked as the ninth largest tire manufacturer, the company successfully boosted revenues from under $900 million as recently as 1990 to an estimated $1.3 billion in 1994.

The company sells 50 percent of its production output under its own Cooper and Falls brand names and the balance under private label customer programs. It targets the tire replacement market, as opposed to the OEM (original equipment manufacturer) market, with tight competition and lower product margins.

Automobile and truck tires and tubes account for 85 percent of annual revenues while the balance comes from industrial rubber products business. Industrial rubber products include hose and hose assemblies, vibration control products, automotive sealing systems, and specialty seating components.

Management Talent. Patrick W. Rooney recently took over the company reins as Chairman and Chief Executive Officer after serving as Cooper Tire & Rubber Company President for a number of years.

Financial Status. The company's financial position, with nearly $29 million in cash and only $38 million in long-term debt, provides operating flexibility. The board of directors raised the cash dividend 9 percent in mid-1994.

Particular Strengths. Cooper has been busy adding to its product line and as a result enlarging and strengthening its customer base. A new 163,000-square-foot tire warehouse adds to capacity and improves distribution service, while a new weather seal and rubber hose facility built in 1993 had its first full year of operation in 1994. Likewise, the company's Piedras Negras molded products plant is expected to capture new Mexican business.

Financial Statistics

($ millions except per-share data)

	1992	*1993*	*1994*
Revenue	1175	1193	1403
Net income (loss)	108*	102	129
Earnings (loss)/share	1.30*	1.22	1.54
Dividends/share	.17	.20	.23
Long-term debt	48	39	34
Stock price range/share:	1992	1993	1994
High	35⅝	39⅝	29½
Low	22⅛	20	21⅝

*Before effects of accounting change in the amount of $65 million or 78 cents per share.

Investment Assessment. Cooper's fundamentals are impressive, with rising revenues and earnings. Strong demand and higher tire prices strengthen prospects for the future, as does a rebounding economy. Automotive manufacturing remains robust, creating increased demand for Cooper's industrial rubber products. The company has scheduled overtime to meet demand. Facility expansion and equipment renovations will add to capacity and improve efficiency.

Fidelity Select Regional Banks Portfolio
12 Devonshire Street
Boston, MA 02109-3605
Telephone: 800-544-8888
Ticker symbol: FSRBX
Investment advisor: Fidelity Management and Research Co.

Year begun: 1986
Assets: $97 million
Load: 3.0 percent maximum
Minimum investment: $2500
Annual expense ratio: 1.60 percent
Turnover: 74 percent

Investment Strategy. Fidelity Select Regional Banks Portfolio seeks quality banks with improving credit quality, good cost control, rising fee income, and a growing loan portfolio for long-term appreciation. Cumulative total returns since inception have outpaced the S&P 500.

Returns

One-year:	−2.7 percent through 12/31/94
Three-year:	17.09 percent through 12/31/94
Five-year:	16.12 percent through 12/31/94

Representative Major Holdings

Company	*Industry*	*HQ*
Citicorp	Money center	New York
Bank of New York Co.	Regional banking	New York
Signet Banking Corp.	Regional banking	Virginia
Bank of Boston Corp.	Regional banking	Massachusetts
NationsBank Corp.	Multiregional	North Carolina
Banc One Corp.	Multiregional	Ohio
First Chicago Corp.	Regional banking	Illinois
State Street Boston	Regional banking	Massachusetts
Boatmen's Bancshares	Regional banking	Missouri
Crestar Financial Corp.	Regional banking	Virginia

Portfolio Composition. Fidelity attempts to stay fully invested in securities of banking institutions, shifting funds from region to region as economic conditions warrant. The Northeast and Midwest regions carried heavier weightings of approximately 25 and 23 percent, respectively, while the Southwest had the lowest concentration of portfolio assets with 1 percent.

Portfolio Holding Evaluation. See the discussion of Zions Bancorporation earlier in this chapter.

Grenada Sunburst System Corporation
2000 Gateway
Grenada, MS 38901

Stock exchange: NASDAQ
Ticker symbol: GSSC
Telephone: 601-226-1100

Company Profile. Grenada Sunburst System Corporation serves the banking needs of customers in Mississippi and, through the 1988 acquisition of Capital Bank in Baton Rouge, Louisiana. Overall, Grenada operates in nearly 60 communities. The company is in its 105th year as a Mississippi financial institution.

Management Talent. Chairman Robert E. Kennington, II and President and Chief Executive Officer James T. Boone have guided Grenada Sunburst through a series of record years. Both have held executive positions within the Grenada Sunburst System for decades.

Financial Status. The company's total assets and loan portfolio have grown dramatically in recent years. Equally important, asset quality has been steadily improving. Nonperforming assets declined from 1.75 percent in 1990 to around .50 percent in 1993. Return on equity rose to 15.56 percent in 1993 from 13.16 percent a year earlier.

Particular Strengths. The $2.4 billion banking company possesses the financial wherewithal to expand both through internal growth and key acquisitions such as the March 1993 $374 million purchase of Eastover Bank for Savings serving over 30,000 customers in 18 Mississippi communities.

Financial Statistics

($ millions except per-share data)

	1992	*1993*
Interest income	144	162
Net income (loss)	18	25
Earnings (loss)/share	2.01	2.70
Dividends/share	.60	.72
Stock price range/share:	1992	1993
High	22	26¾
Low	12¾	19¾

Investment Assessment. Grenada Sunburst was acquired by Union Planters Corporation (NYSE: UPC) on December 31, 1994.

That completes a review of some of the regional funds available to help you round out your hometown and regional investing strategy. Study the various portfolio weightings to see which industry sectors are receiving the most attention. Do the same for track changes in sectors and individual holdings to see which ones are gaining or losing favor with the regional mutual funds so that you can adjust your portfolio accordingly.

A List of Regional Mutual Funds

Mutual funds that specialize in the fortunes of regional companies are a ready source of information. Use them as a handy reference list of potential investment candidates. Request a copy of their prospectuses and most recent annual or semiannual reports. These give you a summary of their investment strategies, views on the regional economy, shifts in investment sectors, and current portfolio holdings. This saves you a lot of investigative work because the funds will already have screened out the companies not positioned to do as well under their investment guidelines.

AmSouth Regional Equity Fund
1900 E. Dublin-Granville Road
Columbus, OH 43229
800-451-8739

Composite Northwest 50 Fund
601 W. Riverside Avenue, Suite 900
Spokane, WA 99201-0694
800-543-8072

First American Regional Equity Fund
680 E. Swedesford Road, No. 7
Wayne, PA 19087-1658
800-637-2548

Growth Fund of Washington, Inc.
1101 Vermont Avenue, NW
Washington, DC 20005-3521
800-421-4120

IAI Regional Fund
601 Second Avenue South
P.O. Box 357
Minneapolis, MN 55402
800-945-3863

Morgan Keegan Southern Capital Fund
50 Front Street, 21st floor
Memphis, TN 38103
800-366-7426

Paragon Gulf South Growth Fund
4900 Sears Tower
Chicago, IL 60606-6391
800-525-7907

Roulston Midwest Growth Fund
4000 Chester Avenue
Cleveland, OH 44103
800-932-7781

SAFECO Northwest Fund, Inc.
SAFECO Plaza
Seattle, WA 98185
800-426-6730

Victory Ohio Regional Stock Fund
Primary Funds Services Corporation
P.O. Box 9741
Providence, RI 02940-9741
800-362-5365

More specialized regional funds cover banking institutions such as:

Fidelity Select Regional Banks Portfolio
12 Devonshire Street
Boston, MA 02109-3605
800-544-8888

Paine Webber Regional Financial Growth Fund, Inc.
1285 Avenue of the Americas, 10th floor
New York, NY 10019
800-647-1568

In the next chapter, we'll take a look at tapping into the research resources of regional brokerage firms and others to uncover attractive hometown investment candidates.

9 Tapping Regional Research Resources

Regional Brokerage Firms

As indicated in Chap. 2, regional brokerage firms represent an excellent avenue to tap into the information pipeline to begin your investigative research on prospective hometown and regional investments. In addition, keeping in touch with your hometown or regional brokerage firm can pay big dividends in terms of being informed of attractive private placements, IPOs, municipal bonds, or other promising investment opportunities.

In the following pages, we will visit a number of regional brokerage firms from across the country. Refer to the end of this chapter for a more complete listing of brokerage firms by each region of the country. Remember that many firms headquartered in one state may have offices in other regions of the country.

Southeast Research Partners, Inc.
2101 Corporate Boulevard, Suite 402
Boca Raton, FL 33431
Telephone: 407-994-9600

Southeast Research Partners is a research boutique that searches out money-making equity ideas mainly, but not exclusively, in the Southeast region of the United States. Its staff of eight analysts have a combined 145 years investment experience. The firm specializes in six major sectors targeted to present attractive investment opportunities in the nineties: consumer, health care, energy, infrastructure/construction, technology, and financial institutions.

Southeast Research Partners covers over 125 companies ranging from major listed corporations to small-cap OTC "special situations." The firm is oriented to the institutional market and serves over 250 major institutional clients in the United States and Canada.

"Following the Peter Lynch principle of investing in what you know and what you are familiar with in your own backyard makes good sense. You can stay one step ahead of Wall Street by being aware of what's happening in your own community or area. Keep posted on new economic activity and company happenings, do your investigative work to satisfy yourself that the investment is sound, and get in early before Wall Street pushes up the price," advises Robert T. McAleer, managing director for Southeast Research Partners.

According to McAleer, regional brokerage and research firms have ready access to company executives in their area. In addition to meeting with them formally at the corporate facilities, more often than not they also have the opportunity to socialize with top management. In other words, the regional analyst can get a far better feel for company management than out-of-town analysts who fly in for several hours or a one-day visit once a quarter or even less frequently.

"Our proximity to regional companies allows us to do more checks than the out-of-town analysts. On top of that, we have the flexibility and opportunity to meet and know other company personnel, which adds another dimension to our analysis that you can't get from outside the area," says McAleer.

A Sampling of Southeast Research Picks

North American Biologicals, Inc.
P.O. Box 692222
1111 Park Centre Boulevard, 3rd floor
Miami, FL 33169

Stock exchange: NASDAQ
Ticker symbol: NBIO
Telephone: 305-625-5303

Industry Review. North American Biologicals, Inc. operates in a unique niche of the biomedical industry, providing plasma and plasma-based products for diagnostic and therapeutic applications, including the prevention and treatment of infectious diseases and immune disorders. A potential new major market for plasma-based products, HIV immune globulin (HIVIG), is being tested for its effectiveness in preventing transmission of the AIDS-causing virus from HIV-positive mothers to unborn infants.

Company Profile. North American Biologicals develops, manufactures, and markets plasma-based health care products. It is the nation's largest provider of plasma-based raw materials, intermediates to the pharmaceutical industry, and produces proprietary plasma-based therapeutics. The company also operates 66 BioMedical Plasma Collection Centers in 29 states plus two centers in Germany. Company-produced special immune globulins are on the market for the prevention or treatment of such diseases as hepatitis-B and rabies.

Management Talent. Chairman, President, and Chief Executive Officer David J. Gury has 30 years' experience in the health care industry. Other top management members possess at least 20 years' experience each. The company recently added David Castaldi, founder and Chief Executive Officer of Bio-Surface Technology, Inc. of Cambridge, Massachusetts, to its Board of Directors. The acquisition of Premier Bioresources, Inc. (PBI) brings on board John C. Carlisle, PBI's founder, who became North American Biologicals' Chief Operating Officer.

Financial Status. Record revenues and earnings work to improve cash flow and working capital to fund new product development and to market share expansion. North American Biologicals enjoys around $14 million in working capital. Long-term debt rose to $21 million in 1994 with the acquisition of Premier Bioresources, Inc., one of the nation's largest independent suppliers of plasma used for human therapeutics. PBI is headquartered in Fort Worth, Texas and generates around $140 million in annual revenues. Part of the proceeds from a late 1994 stock offering were earmarked to retire long-term debt.

Particular Strengths. Key acquisitions are strengthening North American Biologicals' already strong presence in the marketplace. As part of the PBI acquisition, the company has been awarded a five-year contract, valued at $200 million, to supply plasma to Baxter Health Care Corporation. On top of boosting North American Biologicals' annual revenues by 40 percent to $140 million, the acquisition also substantially expands the company's plasma donor base by at least 75 percent short-term and potentially even more long-term.

Financial Statistics

($ millions except per-share data)

	1992	1993	1994
Revenues	84	102	165
Net income/(loss)	(0.6)	3.5	7.9
Earnings (loss)/share	(.04)	.26	.45
Dividends/share	—	—	—
Long-term debt	16	15	20
Stock price range/share:	1992	1993	1994
High	7⅝	9¼	8½
Low	1⅝	4¼	2 15/16

Investment Assessment. North American Biologicals has a lot going for it. The PBI acquisition brought in an expanded plasma donor base and new markets for its products. The June 1994 establishment of a German subsidiary and the acquisition of two German plasma collection facilities expand the company's role in the European market, the second largest in the world. Overall, European sales were expected to contribute 40 percent of company revenues in 1994.

The company is in the process of building a new biopharmaceutical manufacturing facility, scheduled for completion during 1995, geared to vertically integrate all plasma manufacturing processes and enhance productivity. On the earnings front, intensified marketing efforts and the new acquisitions are expected to deliver solid earnings increases for years to come.

Southeast Research Partners sees North American Biologicals' stock trading at 18 to 20 times estimated earnings per share, leading to a long-term target in the $13–$15-per-share range.

Pharmacy Management Services, Inc.
3611 Queen Palm Drive
Tampa, FL 33619

Stock exchange: NASDAQ
Ticker symbol: PMSV
Telephone: 800-237-7676

Industry Review. Pharmacy Management Services, Inc. serves the medical community with cost containment and managed care services. The current drive to reform health care and effect lower costs promises to aid firms such as Pharmacy Management, which can provide cost-effective services. Cost containment efforts are especially acute in the workers' compensation area within which Pharmacy Management operates.

Company Profile. Pharmacy Management Services, Inc. is a major independent nationwide provider of medical cost containment and managed care services in the specialized field of workers' compensation. The company's comprehensive services can provide all of an injured worker's health care needs from the time of the on-the-job injury through return to work or the home care environment. Services include accident and injury reporting, case management, vocational counseling, a preferred provider organization of hospitals, retail prescription drug card, and home delivery of medical supplies and equipment.

Management Talent. Cecil S. Harrell, Chairman and Chief Executive Officer, founded the company in 1972 and has served as its CEO since that time and as Chairman since December 1991. Bertram T. Martin, Jr. joined the firm as President and Chief Operating Officer in June 1993 after having been a vice president of a corporate financial consulting business for eight years, a firm that advised Pharmacy Management Services.

Financial Status. After suffering a loss of 25 cents per share in fiscal year 1992, Pharmacy Management made a strong comeback with earnings of 30 cents per share and 47 cents per share in fiscal years 1993 and 1994, respectively.

Long-term debt has been trimmed substantially in the past two years, dropping from over $18 million at the end of fiscal 1992 to under $6 million at the end of fiscal 1994. Adding to operating flexibility, in the past year working capital improved nearly 30 percent to $16.7 million.

Particular Strengths. Pharmacy Management maintains a broad customer base, serving over 35,000 referring claims representatives in 15,000 claims offices, representing 4000 workers' compensation claims payors. The company ships medical equipment, medical supplies, and prescription drugs to all 50 states from a Tampa, Florida central distribution and warehouse facility.

Cost control and higher margins are improving the firm's bottom line. Earnings rose to 47 cents per share in fiscal 1994, up over 56 percent from fiscal 1993 results. Projections of fiscal 1995 earnings to rise over 100 percent to 85 cents per share were issued after the fiscal year's strong first quarter.

Financial Statistics

($ millions except per-share data)

	Fiscal year ended July 31			
	1993	*1994*	*3 months 1994*	*3 months 1995*
Revenues	110	113	27	30
Net income (loss)	2.8	4.3	.7	1.8
Earnings (loss)/share	.30	.47	.08	.20
Dividends/share	—	—	—	—
Long-term debt	12	6	6	6
Stock price range/share:	1993	1994		
High	9	18½		
Low	4¾	6¼		

Investment Assessment. Investors who followed Southeast Research Partners' May 1994 buy recommendation when the stock traded around $7¼ per share would have profited handsomely. In October, the company went into play as a takeover candidate and the board of directors retained Smith Barney, Inc. as its financial advisor in maximizing the value of the company for its shareholders.

Pharmacy Management Services' stock price soared from a 1994 high of $12 per share in August 1994 to $18½ per share in late November while takeover possibilities ensued.

Robert W. Baird & Company, Inc.
777 East Wisconsin Avenue
Milwaukee, WI 53202
800-792-2473

9202 West Dodge Road
Omaha, NE 68114
800-866-1010

Robert W. Baird & Company, Inc., headquartered in Milwaukee, Wisconsin, maintains 57 offices throughout Florida, Illinois, Indiana, Iowa, Michigan, Minnesota, Nebraska, Ohio, Texas, and Wisconsin. Baird ranks as one of the largest regionally headquartered investment bankers, serving individuals, corporations, municipalities, and institutional investors. Since 1919, the firm has developed a strong presence in and knowledge of the Midwest and has also expanded into major growth markets outside America's Heartland. Its research department is one of the largest between the coasts.

Baird takes a long-term, investment approach in quality companies that it views as rapidly growing, well-managed firms positioned to increase market share in their industries. It also plays an active role in private placements and public offerings as well as municipal securities.

Investing in hometown or regional investments lets the individual investor get a good feel for the company through social and other contacts with management and other company personnel. As a hometown investor, you can see growth happening first-hand.

Periodically Baird offices publish lists of common stock purchase recommendations. These can form an excellent starting point for beginning your investigative work to determine which companies have the best prospects and which individual securities make the most sense for your portfolio, given your investment goals and risk posture. The recommendation list is broken down into investment categories such as high yield, growth, attractive cyclicals, and aggressive commitments. There's something there for everybody.

A Baird recommendation list included MGIC Investment Corporation as a growth pick and Casey's General Stores, Inc. as an aggressive commitment.

Casey's General Stores, Inc.
One Convenience Boulevard
Ankeny, IA 50021-8045

Stock exchange: NASDAQ
Ticker symbol: CASY
Telephone: 515-965-6100

Industry Review. While industry competition heats up in the convenience store industry in major and smaller metropolitan areas, the markets that Casey's General Stores competes in (populations of 5000 to 10,000) are still dominantly serviced by independently owned stores without the financial resources and purchasing clout to compete head to head with Casey's.

Company Profile. Headquartered in Ankeny, Iowa, Casey's General Stores, Inc. knows how to operate successfully in small town America. Casey's first store opened in 1968 in a remodeled three-bay gasoline station in Boone, Iowa. The company went public in 1983 and today operates approximately 900 stores in eight midwestern states, all within 500 miles of the 140,000-square-foot corporate distribution center in Ankeny. The company owns or leases around 78 percent of the stores with the balance franchised. Seventy-five percent of the stores are located in towns with populations under 5000. Casey's also maintains a fleet of 75 tractor trailers and 250 other vehicles for efficient delivery.

Annual revenues broke the $700 million mark in fiscal 1994 ended April 30. Casey's management has targeted having 1000 stores in operation by the end of 1996 generating $1 billion in annual revenue. The stores offer a wide selection of foods, beverages, health and beauty aids, and other non-food items. Overall, some 2500 competitively priced items are carried in the Casey's stores.

Management Talent. Chairman and Chief Executive Officer Donald F. Lamberti heads a skilled management team supported by seasoned veterans manning the front lines. Casey's stresses its internal promotion philosophy, with most district managers and store supervisors having worked their way up through the ranks from store managers.

Financial Status. Casey's treasury includes over $10 million in long-term investments and operations, and stock sales provide adequate capital for store construction.

Particular Strengths. The company's strategy of locating in towns where it doesn't meet stiff competition pays off big for Casey's. The company also pays close attention to cost control and squeezing out operating efficiencies. Casey's stores remain open at least 16 hours per day, seven days a week, typically a lot longer than the independent rival stores in its markets.

Financial Statistics

($ millions except per-share data)

	Fiscal year ended April 30			
	1993	*1994*	*9 months 1994*	*9 months 1995*
Revenues	679	736	553	644
Net income (loss)	13.3	17.6	14.2	19.7
Earnings (loss)/share	.60	.73	.58	.76
Dividends/share	.067	.078	.06	.06
Long-term debt	98	61	61	58
Stock price range/share:	1992	1993	1994	
High	9¾	12⅜	15⅜	
Low	6⅜	7⅜	10⅜	

Investment Assessment. An expanding number of stores, remodeling of older stores, and greater market penetration spell higher revenues and earnings for Casey's with projected earnings per share growth in the 15 percent range over the next three to five years.

Piper Jaffray, Inc.
222 South Ninth Street
Minneapolis, MN 55402-3804
Telephone: 612-342-6000

Piper Jaffray, Inc., headquartered in Minneapolis, takes a regional approach to its research activities and publishes a number of industry and regional research booklets including, but not limited to, *Emerging America, The Informed Investor, Midwest Select,* and *Pacific Northwest Outlook,* all of which are rich sources of information on emerging growth companies and potential investments.

Midwest Select, published quarterly, focuses on coverage of market-leading manufacturing and industrial service companies based in the Midwest that are not widely followed by the investment community. Piper zeros in on small to midcapitalization companies from a value perspective to deliver attractive long-term returns while emphasizing the preservation of capital. Investment criteria include:

- Manufacturing/industrial service orientation with Midwest headquarters location.
- Growing companies holding franchise positions in their markets.
- Long-term earnings growth potential.
- Companies that generate free cash flow.
- Companies run by management with a demonstrated commitment to the long-term interest of its shareholders.
- Opportunities to purchase shares at prices with limited downside risk.
- Lack of active research coverage.

Examples of companies covered by *Midwest Select* include:

- ABC Rail Products Corporation (ABCR), a manufacturer of rail products.
- IDEX Corporation (IEX), a manufacturer of fluid handling and industrial products.
- Landauer, Inc. (LDR), a provider of radiation monitoring services.
- Oshkosh Truck Corporation (OTRKB), a manufacturer of specialized heavy duty vehicles.
- Varlen Corporation (VRLN), an industrial metal products manufacturer.

Pacific Northwest Outlook is published monthly out of Seattle, Washington and provides a review of economic activity in the Northwest area. Its purpose is to highlight key economic variables affecting the region and identify equity and fixed income investment opportunities.

A late 1994 report discussion of the Pacific Northwest economy showed strong commercial real estate activity, a harbinger of better economic fundamentals in the months ahead. National market watchers rank the Portland/Seattle market in the top five commercial real estate markets in the United States despite Boeing's layoffs. In addition, renewed foreign interest in the area portends heightened economic fervor in the future. The area's highly skilled workforce, relatively cheap power, and tax incentives have created interest in a wide variety of industries from food processing to high technology.

The publication includes The Pacific Northwest Value List, featuring what Piper Jaffray Research believes are the very best research ideas on companies headquartered or with significant operations in the Pacific Northwest. Among the Value List companies are:

- Electro Scientific Industries (ESIO), a producer of computer-controlled laser systems.
- Fluke Corporation (FLK), a manufacturer of measuring and testing instrumentation equipment.
- Nordstrom, Inc. (NOBE), a department store featuring upscale merchandise.

Pacific Northwest Outlook also features other up-and-coming companies such as Smith's Food & Drug Centers, Inc. (SFD) and Plum Creek Timber Company, L.P. (PCL). (For a discussion of Plum Creek Timber Company, L.P. refer to Chap. 7.)

A Sampling of Piper Jaffray Picks

Fluke Corporation
P.O. Box 9090
6920 Seaway Boulevard
Seattle, WA 98206

Stock exchange: NYSE
Ticker symbol: FLK
Telephone: 206-347-6100

Industry Review. Fluke Corporation operates in the competitive electronic instrumentation industry. New product development is an essential ingredient to market share and earnings progress. Measuring and testing instrumentation products serve the needs of clients from a wide variety of industries ranging from automotive applications to paper production and building maintenance.

Company Profile. Fluke Corporation took major steps in fiscal 1994 to increase its market presence with the addition of new products and the acquisition of the test and measurement business of Philips Electronics N.V. of the Netherlands, the company's largest acquisition in its 47-year history. The $42 million Philips acquisition, accomplished through a combination of cash and Fluke stock, added $105 million in new annual revenues.

Fluke serves both the domestic and international markets. In fiscal 1994, foreign sales accounted for approximately 53 percent of annual revenues. With the Philips business acquisition, revenues jumped 47 percent in fiscal 1994 to nearly $358 million.

Management Talent. President George Winn and Chief Executive Officer Bill Parzybok, Jr. have introduced the "Phoenix Philosophy" to the organization. It has been instrumental in generating new products and involving the customer early in the product development process. The company is also investing in an enhanced management information system to improve the quality of information used to run the company.

Financial Status. Rising profitability is fueling working capital, which stands in excess of $100 million. In June 1994, the Fluke Board of Directors authorized the repurchase of 150,000 shares of common stock from Philips Electronics N.V. for $4.6 million under its right of first refusal. Long-term debt stands around a very manageable $26 million.

Particular Strengths. During May 1994 Fluke entered a very lucrative market with the introduction of its first measuring and testing tools specifically targeted at the world's critical process industries. In the United States alone, there are 20,000 processing plants with an estimated annual output of $500 billion.

On the international front, business in Mexico doubled in the past five years and stands to benefit from the North American Free Trade Agreement (NAFTA). The Philips acquisition positions Fluke to capture more market share with the eventual recovery of the European economy.

Financial Statistics

($ millions except per-share data)

	Fiscal year ended April			
	1993	*1994*	*9 months 1994*	*9 months 1995*
Revenues	245	358	262	277
Net income (loss)	9.1	8.8	5.7	9.8
Earnings (loss)/share	1.29*	1.10	.71	1.22
Dividends/share	.50	.52	.39	.42
Long-term debt	—	15	15	23
Stock price range/share:	1992	1993	1994	
High	34⅜	30½	32	
Low	23⅜	20¼	24⅝	

*Excluding positive effects of accounting changes totaling $3.9 million or 55 cents per share.

Investment Assessment. Fluke's stock price declined from its 1994 high of $32 per share. However, the long-term prospects of the company are favorable. The stock hit new highs above $40 per share in early 1995.

Smith's Food & Drug Centers, Inc.
1559 South Redwood Road
Salt Lake City, UT 84104

Stock exchange: NYSE
Ticker symbol: SFD
Telephone: 801-974-1400

Industry Review. The Intermountain, Southwestern, and Southern California market areas in which Smith's Food & Drug Centers, Inc. competes are highly competitive, with large regional and national food and drug store chains fighting for market share. Stores that offer customers competitive prices, convenient locations, excellent service, broad product lines of quality merchandise, and clean facilities stand the best chance of outperforming their industry counterparts.

Company Profile. Smith's Food & Drug Centers, Inc. is a leading regional supermarket and drug store chain with over 130 stores in Arizona, California, Idaho, Nevada, New Mexico, Texas, Utah, and Wyoming. The company plans to open 10 to 12 new stores in 1995 and 1996 for further market penetration.

Smith's stores feature modern, attractive layouts carrying a broad range of quality products at competitive everyday low prices combined with quality customer service. During the fourth quarter of 1993, the firm opened a new 1-million-square-foot fully integrated distribution center (including a dairy processing plant) in Riverside, California. Overall, Smith's operates approximately 4.2 million square feet of processing and distribution facilities to service its stores.

Management Talent. Founders Jeffrey P. Smith (Chairman and Chief Executive Officer) and Richard D. Smith (President and Chief Operating Officer) are sacrificing short-term income gains for long-term market position and accompanying earnings potential with an expansive new store program and aggressive pursuit of its everyday low price strategy to attract new customers.

Financial Status. To finance store expansion, Smith's long-term debt has increased nearly $100 million since the end of 1992 to $677 million as of October 1994. In a strategic move, Smith's is scaling back the size of new stores to 54,000–66,000 square feet versus the 75,000-square-foot new stores opened in recent years. As a result, the smaller stores will have a lower break-even point, making the company more cost-competitive.

Particular Strengths. With the exception of California, the company's store locations are enjoying vibrant economies. Strict attention to cost control and operating efficiencies will keep Smith's a tough competitor.

Financial Statistics

($ millions except per-share data)

	1992	*1993*	*1994*
Revenues	2650	2807	2981
Net income (loss)	54	46	49
Earnings (loss)/share	1.79	1.52	1.73
Dividends/share	.44	.52	.52
Long-term debt	592	704	700
Stock price range/share:	1992	1993	1994
High	43¼	37¼	26¾
Low	25¾	19	18⅛

Investment Assessment. Weakness in the California market, stiff price competition in Utah, and new store opening expenses combined to reduce earnings in 1993 and the first half of 1994. As a result, investors took flight, dropping the company's stock price from a high of $43¼ in 1992 to a low of $18⅛ per share in 1994 before rebounding strongly to 52-week highs in 1995. Smith's is setting the stage for long-term revenues and earnings growth.

D. A. Davidson & Company

8 Third Street
Great Falls, MT 59401
406-727-4200
800-332-5915

200 First Avenue East
Kalispell, MT 59903
800-680-6212 (local)
800-955-2208 (national)

D. A. Davidson & Company services its brokerage clients through 18 offices throughout Montana, Idaho, Washington, and Wyoming. It keeps in close contact with interesting investments throughout the region.

Gregory D. Barkus, Vice President and Branch Manager of Davidson's Kalispell, Montana operation, points out that hometown and regional investors get the added satisfaction that investing in these companies provides a return to their community in the form of new jobs, taxes, and community service.

"The investor with a regional focus can get out there and kick the tires and see first-hand how the company's operations are running," says Barkus.

However, Barkus issues an important caveat when considering investing in local or regional companies. "Don't be blinded by the local aspect of the investment. Take a close look at the big picture in terms of economic environment, competition, and market share to decide whether or not the investment makes sense," advises Barkus.

Word of mouth—a personal recommendation—is the highest form of praise. Barkus has earned his share by skillfully placing his clients in money-making investments. For example, Barkus interested Dick Irvin of Columbia Falls, Montana in the spinoff of Plum Creek Timber Company, L.P. from Burlington Resources, Inc. (as discussed in Chap. 4; for an analysis of Plum Creek Timber Company, L.P., see Chap. 7).

Barkus also steered Lewis McBride of Kalispell, Montana into investing in the IPO of Glacier Bancorp, Inc. back in 1984. The investment in the Kalispell bank holding company has been a winner. Since going public, Glacier's stock has performed well in the market. From a low of 1⁹⁄₁₆, the stock hit a high of 23⅛ in 1993—not a bad return from anyone's perspective.

"I purchased a number of shares on Greg's recommendation when Glacier went public and still have 1000 shares. It has been an excellent investment for me. I depend on Greg's investigative work and analysis. He hasn't led me wrong yet," says McBride.

Current Investment Analysis

Glacier Bancorp, Inc.
202 Main Street
Kalispell, MT 59901

Stock exchange: NASDAQ
Ticker symbol: GBCI
Telephone: 406-756-4200

Industry Review. The Northwest Montana economy in which Glacier Bancorp, Inc. operates is healthy, exhibiting record growth.

Company Profile. Glacier Bancorp, Inc. is a multibank, thrift holding company operating through three principal subsidiaries: Glacier Bank FSB with nine offices and a loan origination office, First National Bank of Eureka, and First National Bank Whitefish. The company provides a broad range of retail and commercial banking services as well as full-service brokerage activities.

Management Talent. Chairman and Chief Executive Officer John S. MacMillan has helped guide Glacier Bancorp from a single bank (First Federal Savings Bank of Montana) with $133 million in assets in the mideighties into its present three-bank configuration with a total of $318 million in assets.

Financial Status. For the five-year period ended December 31, 1993, Glacier Bancorp earned a total return of 566.90 percent versus an S&P 500 return of 197.75 percent and a return of 163.15 percent for the 44 banks comprising the Western Bank Monitor (as compiled by Montgomery Securities). In June 1993, the Board of Directors boosted the cash dividend 10 percent and raised it again in December 1993 another 9 percent to 12 cents per share.

Particular Strengths. Glacier Bancorp has a solid foundation in the markets it serves. Mortgage prepayments impacted year-to-year comparisons through the first nine months of 1994, as did the exceptionally strong 1993 first quarter results. Standard & Poor's ranks Glacier A+, the highest rating for common stocks exhibiting growth and stability of earnings and dividends.

Financial Statistics

($ millions except per-share data)

	1992	1993	1994
Net interest income	10	12	14
Net income (loss)	4	5	5
Earnings (loss)/share	1.55	1.87	1.85
Dividends/share	.43	.51	.59
Stock price range/share:	1992	1993	1994
High	16⅛	23⅛	20⅝
Low	8¾	14	15⅞

Revised for stock splits

Investment Assessment. The earnings slowdown and stock market jitters combined to drop Glacier's stock price to the $17-per-share level by the end of November 1994. The company's core business is sound, and the bank will continue to deliver revenue and earnings gains in the years ahead. Purchase for a price rebound and long-term capital appreciation.

Elliott Schlang's *Great Lakes Review*

Mr. Elliott Schlang, CFA/*Great Lakes Review*
Hancock Institutional Equity Services
1111 Chester Avenue
Cleveland, OH 44114
Telephone: 216-621-1330

Elliott Schlang is a man with an eye for value and opportunity. Back in the so-called Rust Bowl days of the Midwest, Schlang launched his investment publication *Great Lakes Review* with the task of ferreting out emerging growth companies and other attractive strategic investments in America's heartland surrounding the Great Lakes.

It took a lot of conviction to tout Midwest companies as enticing investments in the midst of the Rust Bowl mentality so prevalent at the time. But more than that, it took investigative savvy to compile the enviable track record that Schlang and his *Great Lakes Review* have earned.

From inception in 1981 through December 31, 1993, The Review's 83 recommendations gained an average 111 percent versus only 55 percent for a weighted index comprised of the Dow Jones Industrial Average, S&P

500, and NASDAQ Composite. The average holding period stood at three years and two months. Sixty-six percent of the recommendations advanced, 27 percent declined, and 7 percent were unchanged.

Schlang searches out these companies early enough to establish a position to capitalize as price/earnings ratios for the companies rise in line with broadening investor interest in the performance of the firms.

"There are always attractive investment opportunities no matter where the market is or where the economy is headed. We search out the best-quality companies at the right prices," says Schlang.

Schlang investment criteria include, but are not limited to:

- Emerging growth companies with consistent earnings growth in excess of inflation.
- High return on equity and sales.
- Self-funding balance sheet.
- Limited foreign exposure.
- Little institutional ownership.
- Flexible labor policies.
- Heavy insider ownership.

"There's no substitute for management ownership. That entrepreneurial drive is crucial. We like to 'live' with management a bit before we add them to our list," says Schlang.

Schlang also stresses the importance of diversification. Despite *Great Lakes*' overall impressive gains, 27 percent of the recommendations have declined. (See Chap. 4 for an in-depth discussion of diversification and investment risk.)

In addition to its list of recommendations, *Great Lakes Review* also periodically profiles other investment possibilities for consideration.

RPM, Inc.
2628 Pearl Road
P.O. Box 777
Medina, OH 44258

Stock exchange: NASDAQ
Ticker symbol: RPOW
Telephone: 216-273-5090

RPM has been a core *Review* holding for many years. In my Money Book Club Main Selection for 1995, *The 105 Best Investments for the 21st Century* (McGraw-Hill, 1995), I featured RPM, Inc. as one of the 105 best investments for the twenty-first century and as a major investment club holding highlighted in my Money Book Club Selection, *Main Street Beats Wall Street* (Probus, 1995).

Industry Review. RPM, Inc. operates in two major markets: specialty chemicals for the industrial maintenance industry and do-it-yourself consumer products. The never ending battle to preserve the world's buildings and infrastructure delivers growth for RPM, as does the expansion of the consumer do-it-yourself segment.

Company Profile. RPM, Inc. manufactures coatings, sealants, and specialty chemicals for industrial and consumer markets worldwide. Its industrial products are used in general maintenance, corrosion control, waterproofing, and other applications. Its do-it-yourself consumer products serve the automotive repair, hobby, home maintenance, leisure, and marine market segments. RPM's products are sold in over 100 countries and manufactured at 45 facilities in the United States, Belgium, Canada, Luxembourg, and the Netherlands. Foreign business generates approximately 12 percent of annual revenues.

RPM excels at purchasing companies with specialized products and unique market niches, and it works hard to improve its operating efficiencies and marketing thrust. RPM takes a unique approach to acquisitions. Instead of replacing management of the acquired company, RPM prefers to keep them running the company, under RPM guidelines and with salaries tied to incentive performance benchmarks.

Management Talent. Chairman and Chief Executive Officer Thomas C. Sullivan and President and Chief Operating Officer James A. Karman have a track record of dozens of successful acquisitions to propel RPM revenues and earnings growth.

Financial Status. RPM has plenty of working capital and credit facilities to continue its aggressive growth through acquisition policy. In October 1994 the Board of Directors boosted the cash dividend by 8 percent to 14 cents per share quarterly. RPM has boosted its cash dividend for 20 straight years. Forty-seven years of consecutive record revenues, net income, and earnings per share keep RPM's finances in excellent order.

Particular Strengths. Strong finances, growing markets, and improved performance turned in by acquisitions all power RPM's impressive performance.

Financial Statistics

($ millions except per-share data)

	Fiscal year ended April 30			
	1993	*1994*	*9 months 1994*	*9 months 1995*
Revenues	768	816	598	737
Net income (loss)	40	53	36	41
Earnings (loss)/share	.74	.93	.63	.72
Dividends/share	.47	.51	.39	.52
Long-term debt	259	233	233	413
Stock price range/share:	1992	1993	1994	
High	18½	19⅜	19⅝	
Low	12⅝	16¼	16¼	

Investment Assessment. RPM broke the ranks of the Fortune 500 based on results through fiscal year ended May 31, 1993. It ranked 491st based on sales but 104th in return on sales, 111th in return on shareholder's equity, and 87th in return to shareholders over a ten-year period.

A 1000-share purchase of RPM stock back in 1974 at $10 per share would have been worth over $700,000 by the end of fiscal 1994, paying out $21,000 in annual cash dividends. A 1000-share investment in 1984 at $16 per share would be worth approximately $90,000 today with a cash dividend payout of $2600 annually.

Looking ahead, the fiscal 1994 acquisitions of Stonehard, Inc. and Dynatron/Bondo, plus the fiscal 1995 acquisition of Rust-Oleum Corporation, add nearly $250 million in annual revenues. Rust-Oleum complements RPM's already strong presence in the do-it-yourself market as well as in its industrial segment.

Stonehard, the worldwide leader in industrial and commercial polymer flooring, gives RPM an entry into this new market. Dynatron/Bondo, a manufacturer of automotive repair coatings, provides synergistic benefits with RPM's consumer automotive product lines.

RPM is poised to deliver more record results in 1995 and beyond. Purchase for long-term capital appreciation.

Use your local and regional brokerage firms to your best advantage to discover intriguing investment opportunities and earn exceptional returns. The following list of firms with local and regional twists will get you started. There are nearly 1000 local and regional brokerage firms. For a complete listing, refer to *The National Directory of Addresses and Telephone Numbers*, published by Omnigraphics, Inc. in Detroit, Michigan.

A Listing of Brokerage Firms

East

Advest Group, Inc.
280 Trumbull Street
Hartford, CT 06103
203-525-1421

Barclay Investments, Inc.
50 South Main Street
Providence, RI 02903
401-272-9690

Alex. Brown & Sons, Inc.
135 East Baltimore Street
Baltimore, MD 21202
410-727-1700

Boenning & Scattergood, Inc.
4 Falls Corporate Center, Suite 212
West Conshohocken, PA 19428
610-832-1212

Hazlett Burt & Watson, Inc.
1300 Chaplin Street
Wheeling, WV 26003
304-233-3312

Janney Montgomery Scott, Inc.
1601 Market Street, 18th floor
Philadelphia, PA 19103
215-665-6000

Legg Mason Wood Walker, Inc.
111 South Calvert Street
Baltimore, MD 21202
410-539-3400

Sage Rutty & Company
183 East Main Street
Rochester, NY 14604
716-232-3760

Troster Singer Corporation
10 Exchange Place, 9th floor
Jersey City, NJ 07302
201-332-2285

Tucker, Anthony, Inc.
200 Liberty Street
New York, NY 10281
212-225-8000

South

J. C. Bradford & Company
330 Commerce Street
Nashville, TN 37201-1809
615-748-9000

Brown Baxter & Company
248 East Capitol Street, Suite 1110
Jackson, MS 39201
601-948-8841

Dorsey & Company, Inc.
511 Gravier Street
New Orleans, LA 70130
504-524-5431

Interstate/Johnson Lane Corp.
121 West Trade Street
Charlotte, NC 28202
704-379-9000

Raymond James & Associates, Inc.
880 Carillon Parkway
St. Petersburg, FL 33733-2749
813-578-3800

Morgan Keegan & Company, Inc.
50 Front Street
Memphis, TN 38103
901-524-4100

Norris Edgar M. & Company
15 South Main Street
Greenville, SC 29601
803-233-3655

Porter White & Yardley, Inc.
P.O. Box 12367
Birmingham, AL 35202
205-252-3681

Robinson-Humphrey Company, Inc.
3333 Peachtree Road, NE
Atlanta, GA 30326
404-266-6000

Wheat First Securities
901 East Byrd Street
Richmond, VA 23211-1357
804-649-2311

Midwest

Robert W. Baird & Co., Inc.
777 East Wisconsin Avenue, 26th floor
Milwaukee, WI 53202
800-792-2473

William Blair & Company
135 South LaSalle Street
Chicago, IL 60603
800-621-9687

Blunt Ellis & Loewi, Inc.
111 East Kilbourn Avenue
Milwaukee, WI 53202
414-347-3400

The Chicago Corporation
208 South LaSalle Street, Suite 200
Chicago, IL 60604
800-621-0686

A. G. Edwards & Sons, Inc.
One North Jefferson
St. Louis, MO 63103
314-289-3000

Inter-Regional Financial Group, Inc.
Dain Bosworth, Inc.
100 Dain Tower
Minneapolis, MN 55402
612-371-7750

Edwards D. Jones & Company
201 Progress Parkway
Maryland Heights, MO 63043
314-851-2000

McDonald & Company Securities, Inc.
800 Superior Avenue, Suite 2100
Cleveland, OH 44114
216-443-2300

The Ohio Company
155 East Broad Street
Columbus, OH 43215
614-464-6811

Piper Jaffray & Hopwood, Inc.
222 South Ninth Street
Minneapolis, MN 55440
612-342-6000

Southwest Securities, Inc.
1201 Elm Street, Suite 4300
Dallas, TX 75270
214-651-1800

Stephens, Inc.
111 Center Street
Little Rock, AR 72203
800-643-9691

Waddell & Reed, Inc.
6300 Lamar
Shawnee, KS 66202
913-236-2000

Ziegler Company, Inc.
215 North Main Street
West Bend, WI 53095
414-334-5521

West

Black & Company, Inc.
1 SW Columbia Street
Portland, OR 97258
503-248-9600

Boettcher & Company, Inc.
828 Seventeenth Street
Denver, CO 80202
800-525-3286

D. A. Davidson & Company
Davidson Building
Great Falls, MT 59401
800-332-5915

Dickinson & Company
2425 East Camelback, Suite 530
Phoenix, AZ 85016
602-957-1951

Hambrecht & Quist, Inc.
One Bush Street
San Francisco, CA 94104
415-576-3300

Interpacific Investors Services, Inc.
1 Union Square, Suite 2310
Seattle, WA 98101
206-623-2784

Jeffries & Company, Inc.
11100 Santa Monica Boulevard, 10th floor
Los Angeles, CA 90025
310-445-1199

Montgomery Securities
600 Montgomery Street
San Francisco, CA 94111
415-627-2000

Pacific Crest Securities
1100 SW 6th Avenue, Suite 1500
Portland, OR 97204
503-248-0721

Yeager Securities, Inc.
16633 Ventura Boulevard, Suite 1220
Encino, CA 91436
818-377-6300

10
Venturing into Business

There are numerous ways to stake your claim in a business enterprise or two without purchasing the stock of publicly traded companies on an organized stock exchange. In this chapter, we delve into a number of such options, including becoming an angel, organizing a small business investment company, investing in a venture capital fund, and providing venture capital.

Becoming an Angel

Who wouldn't like to attain angel status? You don't have to wait until you reach heaven, however. You can begin right here on earth. In the business world, an angel is a person who backs entrepreneurial companies during start-up, second- or third-tier financing, and/or expansion phases. Of course, most earthbound angels don't give money to fledgling companies purely out of the kindness of their hearts. Instead, they acquire an interest in the company in exchange for their financial backing. This can take a variety of forms or combinations of common stock, preferred stock, debt with equity kickers, and warrants.

Let's put the angel business into perspective. An estimated 500,000 small entrepreneurial American companies raise about $50 billion annually from financial angels. Without a doubt, angels are big business—but how profitable is the angel business?

Obviously, angeling has its share of business risks since much of the financing deals are with start-up or early-stage companies (with high failure rates). Many of the products or ideas have yet to be proven in the marketplace. And many of the entrepreneurs possess the product or technical knowledge but lack financial and management expertise to properly run a business.

Despite the risks, there are substantial opportunities for significant investment gains after proper analysis of the venture. The experience of the following two angels clearly illustrates the investment gain potential of becoming an angel to local and regional entrepreneurial companies.

Angel Malachi Mixon III

Malachi Mixon III of Elyria, Ohio (Chairman, President, and CEO of Invacare Corporation, the world's leading manufacturer of home health care equipment) has grown his company from $19 million to $410 million in 15 years, going public in 1984. As a hobby, Mixon serves as an angel to many Cleveland, Ohio area entrepreneurs.

Mixon saw an opportunity to clean up with an investment in Cleveland-based Royal Appliance Manufacturing Company, the maker of the Dirt Devil vacuum cleaners and other household appliances.

In this LBO, Mixon received a 10 percent ownership stake in Royal Appliance for his $20,000 investment in 1981. Ten years later, the company went public and Angel Mixon had parlayed his original $20,000 into $30 million.

Mixon has invested in a number of Northeast Ohio firms looking for capital including:

- CenCor, Inc., a temporary employment service company.
- AccuSpray, a paint spray gun manufacturer.
- STERIS, a manufacturer of medical sterilization equipment.

What does it take to convince Mixon to become an angel? "First and foremost, I look at the entrepreneur. I ask myself, 'Does he or she have the talent, drive, and ambition to carry off the deal to make the business a success? What is their experience and track record of success in past ventures?'" offers Mixon.

Mixon also stresses that it's important to decide if the personal chemistry works. After all, they will be using your money to run their business. The working relationship must therefore be such that you feel comfortable with the level of detail and candor you will be getting from the people in whom you are investing. Some angels prefer a hands-off approach while others possess business expertise and networking contacts that could prove beneficial to the firm and its success. Make sure your expectations and those of the people running the business match to prevent hard feelings and trouble down the road.

Angels must also pay close attention to the business concept itself. Does it really make economic sense or is it a pipe dream? What vision does the person have for the business in the long term? What plans are set in place to achieve that vision? How will the angel's financial backing be put to use—to fund research and development, to increase marketing efforts, or to pad officer salaries?

Finally, does a viable exit strategy exist to allow the angel to leave with his or her principal intact plus a respectable investment gain? In the Mixon/Royal Appliance financing arrangement, an initial public offering was anticipated from the outset of the deal.

Not everything goes as planned. As Mixon puts it, "There are a lot of horror stories out there." But careful character assessment, project analysis, and detailed planning can help tilt the odds in your favor.

Angel Zane D. Showker

Zane D. Showker, Chairman Emeritus of Sysco Virginia (part of Houston, Texas–based food distribution and service giant Sysco Corporation) believes in fostering the entrepreneurial spirit and giving back to the community. Over the years he has funded the Entrepreneurship Chair at James Madison University in his hometown of Harrisonburg, Virginia, as well as invested and started a number of businesses such as a regional telephone company and a Lincoln/Mercury automobile dealership he felt would be beneficial to Harrisonburg.

"I like to invest in businesses I can drive by and see what's happening. It's a gut feeling that tells you whether or not things are going right," says Showker.

Showker likes to purchase or invest in businesses that someone else will run so that he can concentrate on the "bottom right hand corner" of the income statement.

"The manager or business owner must have a passion for the business," stresses Showker.

He invested in a local commercial printing business that had a negative $10 per share book value—a classic turnaround situation with the right manager. Showker knew from first-hand knowledge that the area needed the services of a quality commercial printer. The manager turned the company around, and the firm's book value now stands at $200 per share.

Another Showker investment didn't go quite as planned. According to Showker, despite significant investment, the local telephone company drudged along for some five years without generating any significant profit for its shareholders to show as a return on their investment. However, during those five years, the telephone company continued to expand its customer base. The owners explored the possibility of selling the local telephone company to a larger telecommunications firm. The result: Showker's original $50,000 investment grew to $350,000.

Tapping into the Angel Network

Networking is crucial to finding out about promising businesses in which to invest. The following leads can get you in the right spot at the right time.

- Bankers, attorneys, accountants, and consultants (See the angel profile below.)
- Investment bankers (Study the prospectuses of companies going public to determine who the deal makers are.)
- Industry trade organizations
- Business leaders
- Community, area, and state economic development managers
- Advertisements (yours and theirs)
- Venture capital clubs
- Professional service providers that charge businesses a finder's fee (Typically angel investors pay nothing.)

The Seed Capital Network, Inc. in Knoxville, Tennessee matches entrepreneurs and angels who belong to the Network's client-investor pool. This network selected private investors from a pool of investors who participated in a pilot private business finance project sponsored by the U.S. Small Business Administration. These investors stand ready to invest between $5000 to $1.5 million in ideas, products, or markets with growth potential. The investment from Seed Capital Network investor-clients averages nearly $600,000, which may come from more than one investor.

These networks are springing up all over the country. Check with your local or area community college or university. The entrepreneurial department can put you in touch with the network or networks closest to your city.

Do you fit the angel profile? Check yourself out with the angel characteristics compiled by James Arkebauer, President of Venture Associates, an investment banking and consulting firm in Denver, Colorado, cofounder and chairman of the Rockies Venture Club, and author of *Ultrapreneuring* (McGraw-Hill, 1994).

Arkebauer's Angel Characteristics

- Is between 40 and 60 years of age.
- Ninety percent probability of being male.
- Holds a master or multiple advanced degrees.
- Possesses prior start-up experience.
- Has personal income between $100,000 and $250,000 annually.
- Invests a minimum of once a year, an average of 2½ times.
- Invests $25,000 to $50,000 per deal, totaling $130,000 per year.
- Rarely takes more than 10 percent of a deal.
- Seeks a minimum 20 percent compound annual return.
- Expects to exit in five to seven years.
- Has a strong preference for manufacturing deals.
- Prefers familiar technology.
- Prefers start-ups, early-stage companies.
- Dislikes moderate growth.
- Likes the consulting role—board of directors/advisors.
- Likes to invest with other sophisticated investors.
- Invests close to home (within a 50- to 300-mile radius).
- The primary investment motivation is a high rate of return.
- Secondary motivation is capital appreciation.
- Learns of investment opportunities from associates and friends.
- Less than 30 percent of referrals come from attorneys or accountants.
- Refers investments made to investment network.
- Would like to see more opportunities than he or she currently sees.

The financing arrangement or amount of equity or equity kickers you get in the business is negotiable, but it depends to a large extent on the amount of capital you put up, the upside potential, the downside risks, and your negotiating skills.

Small Business Investment Company Program (SBIC)

To foster investment in start-up companies and to encourage economic growth, the United States Small Business Administration (SBA) launched the SBIC Program in 1958. Essentially, SBICs are venture capital firms licensed by the SBA, designed to augment private capital sources to start-up and growing firms by using government guarantees to borrow funds.

The SBICs are privately owned and managed investment firms that use their funds, augmented by funds borrowed at favorable rates with an SBA guarantee and/or by selling the SBIC's preferred stock to the SBA.

Any company, limited partnership, or limited liability company formed solely for the purpose of operating as a licensee under the Small Business Investment Act may apply for a license. It must be domiciled in the United States. The basic requirement is that the SBIC must have sufficient private capital and management expertise to be operated soundly. The absolute minimum capital established by law for the licensing of new SBICs is $2.5 million. However, in practice, an SBA review typically requires at least $5 million in initial capital as the smallest feasible amount.

The SBA publishes a *Directory of Operating Small Business Investment Companies.* It can prove to be a rich networking source. To receive a copy or to request information on establishing an SBIC, contact the SBA at Associate Administrator for Investment, U.S. Small Business Administration, 409 Third Street SW, Washington, DC 20416, or call the SBA Answer Desk at 800-827-5722.

Renaissance Capital Group, Inc.

Firms like Renaissance Capital Group, Inc. serve two purposes:

1. To provide new capital for growing companies.
2. To deliver superior returns for investors through the mutual fund pooled investment approach.

The principals of Renaissance and its advisors, combined, have over 200 years of experience in evaluating, financing, investing in, and advising growth companies.

Each fund's portfolio contains a diversified stable of emerging growth companies. Investments are targeted in publicly traded companies that have a five-year or longer record of operating performance, a highly successful management team, and products or services that have a forecastable growth rate in excess of 20 percent over the next seven years.

Favorable tax treatment represents another potential investment benefit. Under the 1993 tax legislation, investors receive a 50 percent reduction in capital gains tax by investing directly in American companies with assets under $50 million and holding the investment for five years. Depending on the securities held by the funds, this tax break may be available to fund shareholders.

To date, Renaissance has initiated three different funds. As of December 31, 1993, the fair value of the Renaissance Capital Partners, Ltd. Fund (a limited partnership begun in mid-1990) totaled $18.9 million compared to a cost basis of $10.7 million, for a whopping 77 percent gain. One of the major winners for Renaissance is its $800,000 investment in MaxServ, Inc., an Austin, Texas–based information services firm focusing on the delivery of information regarding the repair, care, and operation of home appliances and electronics to service technicians and consumers. Renaissance's MaxServ investment had grown to over $3 million at the end of 1993 and to over $4 million at the end of November 1994. (See following discussion of MaxServ.)

Other Renaissance Capital Partners, Ltd. Fund portfolio holdings include:

- Biopharmaceuticals, Inc. (a producer of private label and proprietary pharmaceutical products).
- CEL Communications, Inc. (interactive video and documentary films).
- Global Environmental Corporation (industrial air cleaning and specialty manufacturing).
- International Movie Group, Inc. (movie distribution).
- SelecTronics, Inc. (electronic publishing).
- Unico, Inc. (direct advertising).

Renaissance's third fund, Renaissance Capital Growth & Income Fund III, Inc., has been fully subscribed at $40 million and will start trading as a closed-end mutual fund during 1995, most likely on NASDAQ. This fund will target microcap stocks, public companies with market capitalizations of between $10 million to $100 million.

Portfolio Holding Evaluation

MaxServ, Inc.
8317 Cross Park Drive, Suite 350
Austin, TX 78754

Stock exchange: NASDAQ
Ticker symbol: MXSV
Telephone: 512-834-8341

Industry Review. The information services industry continues to explode with the proliferation of personal computers, both in the business and consumer environments. While many companies provide business information services, there is no known direct competitor with the comprehensive technical library of MaxServ.

Company Profile. MaxServ, Inc. provides information services nationwide to manufacturers, retailers, servicers, and consumers engaged in the repair and servicing of a variety of products including appliances, personal computers, consumer electronics, lawn and garden equipment, exercise equipment, and heating and air conditioning equipment.

The company provides support mainly through 800 and some 900 telephone support centers utilizing an extensive library of technical information fully integrated with a sophisticated computer system of databases, including a diagnostic database developed, maintained, and enhanced by the company. A leading information services company, MaxServ focuses on the delivery of repair and maintenance information to service technicians and consumers. MaxServ responds to 4 million information requests on over 200 products brands annually.

Management Talent. President and Chief Executive Officer Charles F. Bayless and his management team have expanded MaxServ from eight employees in 1989 to over 675 repair technicians, parts specialists, customer service representatives, information technology professionals, and managers.

Financial Status. Increasing earnings and cash flow have provided MaxServ with adequate capital to continue software development and expand its operations. During fiscal 1994, the company invested approximately $1.7 million in capital equipment, substantially funded from operating cash flow.

Under the terms of the company's unsecured convertible notes payable in the amount of $800,000, the holder converted the notes outstanding into 1,066,667 shares of company common stock, thus completely eliminating the firm's convertible notes payable obligation.

Particular Strengths. MaxServ's relationship with Sears, Roebuck and Company provides a locked-in major client (in fiscal 1994 Sears accounted for 92 percent of the company's annual revenues). While depending on one company for a majority of annual revenues clearly carries a degree of risk, MaxServ's relationship with Sears is strengthening.

In September 1994, the company signed a five-year agreement with Sears Canada, Inc. to convert that company's parts information paper document database into an image and text database. MaxServ will publish and distribute the parts information on CD-ROM. This follows on the heels of MaxServ providing similar services for Sears Product Services in the United States in 1993.

In October 1994, MaxServ and Sears agreed for MaxServ to acquire the assets of and perform sales order services for Sears Product Services Teleparts business and to provide additional information services to Sears Product Services technicians under a long-term service contract. Under the terms of the agreement, Sears will receive 2.3 million shares of MaxServ common stock. Also, Sears will make a $4.5 million investment in MaxServ for an additional 1 million shares of common stock. The move bolsters MaxServ's position in the information services industry.

Financial Statistics

($ thousands except per-share data)

	Fiscal year ended May 31			
	1993	*1994*	*9 months 1994*	*9 months 1995*
Revenues	7420	15,699	11,194	20,258
Net income (loss)	271*	710**	487**	956
Earnings (loss)/share	.07*	.10**	.07**	.11
Dividends/share	—	—	—	—
Long-term debt†	1207	271	271	225
Stock price range/share:	1992	1993	1994	
Low	.25	.87	2.25	
High	1.50	3.75	6.50	

*Excludes effect of extraordinary credit from tax loss carryforward amounting to $144,000 or 4 cents per share.

**Excludes effect of positive change from accounting change totaling $735,000 or 11 cents per share.

†Includes obligations under capital leases.

NOTE: In fiscal 1994 there were substantially more outstanding shares of common stock than in fiscal 1993 (7,950,158 vs. 4,964,621).

Investment Assessment. Significant positives are the facts that Sears continues to increase its business relationship with MaxServ (delivering a stronger revenue base) and that it's enlarging its financial stake in the firm (Sears now owns 65 percent of MaxServ's common stock). In addition, Sears' move to open more scaled-down outlets emphasizing white goods (household appliances), televisions, etc. also means increased revenue opportunities for MaxServ.

For the first three quarters of fiscal 1995, MaxServ scored record revenues. Look for more revenues and earnings advances as the new Sears agreement starts to deliver more business in the quarters ahead. Purchase for long-term capital appreciation. This is also a stock that trades very thinly at times and makes for some interesting investment opportunities to pick the stock up cheaply. For example, in late November 1994 only 200 shares traded hands one day and the stock was purchased at a price more than 11 percent lower than it traded at the previous day. (See Chap. 7.)

Venture Capital

On the other end of the spectrum from the financial angels are venture capital firms that invest large sums of money in start-up or expanding businesses. Again, numerous networks of venture capital clubs across the country represent excellent opportunities for making the right contacts. In many cases, the lines between angels and venture capital firms fade. Overall, the following information applies both to individual angels and to more formal venture capital firms.

Like most other business ventures, venture capital has gone high-tech with on-line matching of business start-ups with people and organizations with capital to invest. For example, American Venture Capital Exchange in Portland, Orgeon links approximately 300 investors with over 200 small business opportunities.

A pioneer in matching entrepreneurs with sources of capital, the nonprofit Technological Capital Network at MIT in Cambridge, Massachusetts maintains a database of investors with over $40 million to invest.

Some on-line venture capital services provide the ability to let the investor tap into the system on-line with his or her own computer modem. The electronic database provides capsule summaries on the companies seeking financing, their business plan, financial projections, management experience, and amount of capital required. When a company attracts an investor's attention, he or she can request more detailed information and/or schedule a meeting to investigate the company further.

Depending on the venture capital service, there are typically annual fees for business owners to be listed in the database and sometimes fee charges to the investor as well. The following are a sampling of the venture capital network services available:

American Venture Capital Exchange
Portland, OR
800-292-1993

Business Opportunities Online
Atlantic Highlands, NJ
800-872-8710

Georgia Capital Network
Atlanta, GA
404-894-5344

Kentucky Investment Capital Network
Frankfort, KY
502-564-4252

Mid-Atlantic Investment Network
College Park, MD
301-405-2144

MIT Technology Capital Network
Cambridge, MA
617-253-7163

Northwest Capital Network
Portland, OR
503-282-6273

Pacific Venture Capital Network
Irvine, CA
714-509-2990

Private Investor Network
Aiken, SC
803-648-6851

The Texas Capital Network
Austin, TX
512-794-9398

Uniform Capital Access Network
Research Triangle Park, NC
919-544-4959

Venture Capital Network
St. Paul, MN
612-223-8663

Washington Investment Network
Seattle, WA
206-464-6282

As you can see, many of these venture capital network services have sprung up near universities. Check with the university closest to you to see what they have to offer.

Many of the venture capital networks and venture capital clubs sponsor programs to link up potential investors and companies seeking capital. As an example, the College Park, Maryland Mid-Atlantic Venture Capital Network periodically holds venture capital conferences.

In Denver, The Rockies Venture Club provides a variety of venues to get investors and businesses together. During November 1994, the club sponsored a financing forum as a one-stop marketplace for business funding opportunities. It featured companies looking for capital, venture capital service providers, and investment bankers and other financing sources.

During regular monthly meetings, The Rockies Venture Club features 12-minute presentations by the CEOs of emerging growth companies, 5-minute presentations by companies seeking financing, a keynote speaker discussing various topics of interest to entrepreneurs, and networking time before and after the meeting and presentations. The club also publishes a club directory. The Rockies Venture Club can be contacted at 190 East Ninth Avenue, Suite 370, Denver, CO 80203, or call 303-831-4174.

There are a number of information sources on the intriguing world of venture capital and learning the ropes of venture capital investing. The following venture capital contacts from around the nation should whet your appetite enough to seek out additional venture capital information close to home.

The *J. L. Kellogg Graduate School of Management* at Northwestern University in Evanson, Illinois sponsors a seminar on The Art of Venturing annually. To receive a program brochure contact Executive Programs, J. L. Kellogg Graduate School of Management, Northwestern University, James L. Allen Center, Evanston, IL 60208-2800, or call 708-467-7000.

In October 1994, the *Investment Management Institute* sponsored the Management of Wealth Forum, covering topics such as private investing to create value, closely held businesses, and transfering wealth. The Investment Management Institute can be reached at 342 Madison Avenue, Suite 1602, New York, NY 10173.

The *International Venture Capital Institute* publishes the following informative resources for the venture capitalist:

- *1995 IVCI Directory of Venture Networking Groups (Clubs) and Other Resources:* Covers over 200 venture capital networking groups and over 275 other resource organizations in the United States and Canada ($19.95).
- *1995 IVCI Directory of Business Incubators and University Research & Science Parks:* Contains contact persons at 940 business incubators, university research parks, and science parks in the United States and Canada ($19.95).
- *1994 IVCI Directory of Venture Capital Seed and Early-Stage Funds:* A new directory of over 225 venture capital firms providing seed and/or early stage financing.

The International Venture Capital Institute may be contacted at P.O. Box 1333, Stamford, Connecticut 06904 or call 203-323-3143.

The National Association of Venture Capitalists publishes a list of its members. Information about the association can be obtained from 1655 North Meyer Drive, Suite 700, Arlington, VA 22209.

Pratt's Guide to Venture Capital Sources lists all venture capital sources by state and includes a listing of contact persons. Found in many local and university libraries, it is published by Venture Economics, 40 West 57th Street, New York, NY 10019.

Who's Who in Venture Capital, by A. David Silver, is also available in many libraries. It includes a listing of venture capitalists complete with information on the average size of investment, size of fund, investment criteria, and contact person. It is published by John Wiley & Sons, Inc., 605 Third Avenue, New York, NY 10158.

International Capital Resources, USA publishes the *California Investment Review,* a listing of developmental stage ventures for the private equity investor. Its profiles of investment opportunities include a description of the venture's industry, location, stage of development, management team, product or service, funding to date, and capital requirements.

Although called *California Investment Review,* it covers opportunities in other states. For information contact the publication at 388 Market Street, Suite 500, San Francisco, CA 94111, or call 415-296-2519.

Essentials for Successful Venture Capital Investing

A number of "musts" need to be in place for you to properly evaluate a business venture and succeed in venture capital investing. These form the foundation for thorough analysis and help you make an informed judgment about a specific project's merits, strengths, weaknesses, risks, and potential investment gains. Some of the items may be combined in a comprehensive business plan or proposal, or they may be presented as separate documents. The main point is that all the key pieces of information required to make an objective decision must be at your disposal.

1. You should see a well thought-out business plan detailing the overall business concept, business niche, and marketing strategy.
2. Current financial statements in sufficient detail to reflect operating department expenses, overhead, and profit centers are essential—at least three years of operating history and preferably five years for expansion financing.
3. Look for realistic operating and financial projections for the next three to five years—not "pie-in-the-sky" guestimates but solid estimates backed by a written description of the assumptions used to generate the numbers. Two or three operating or production levels, including a worst case scenario, are preferable.
4. Key management background and experience make up the crux of any successful business venture. Good ideas are a dime a dozen but having the right management team in place can mean the difference between failure, mediocre success, and outstanding investment returns. Look at prior experience and achievements. Evaluate the motivation level of key players. Finally, assess their integrity. Ask yourself, "Is this someone whose business I would be proud to be associated with?"
5. An in-depth analysis of the industry should include a review of major competitors and suppliers, as well as a discussion of how the product will compete against existing and potential products. A projection of the industry fundamentals in terms of projected economic activity in the three to five years ahead is also needed.
6. Get a description of previous and other planned financing, along with a discussion on precisely how your investment capital is to be spent and why.
7. What is the rate of return expected on your investment?
8. Agree on a plan for how you will be kept appraised of the progress of the company. In other words, are you a passive investor requiring only

periodic financial and operating statements or a hands-on investor with a position on the board of directors or advisory board? Is there an early warning system established to alert management and investors before it's "too late"?

9. A preplanned exit from the venture is another must. Is the company planning on going public five years down the road? What exit arrangements have been considered, and how will they be structured?

Orion Corporate Funding, Inc.

Orion Corporate Funding, Inc., an investment banking firm in Englewood, Colorado, represents clients in mergers and acquisitions as well as in debt placement and equity financing. Examples of recent investment activity involving area Colorado firms include $750,000 in bridge financing for an integrated food processor, a $1.5 million equity placement for a gaming firm, and a $2.6 million equity placement for a manufacturer of process controls.

"We seek enhanced returns through investments in companies with a well developed corporate strategy and strong, experienced management. We take an active role in management strategies," says Douglas Nutt, President of Orion Corporate Funding, Inc.

Orion's capital commitments range from $250,000 to the $2.5 million level. Investments are typically structured with convertible debt, preferred stock, or common stock. To finalize a deal, Orion seeks capital from a variety of sources including commercial banks, other investment bankers, and private investors.

There's more than one way to invest in the venture capital arena. Check out the ones that make the most sense from your investment and risk perspective. Then get to work situating yourself in the information pipeline so that you can take advantage of the next intriguing opportunity to boost your investment returns.

Other Ways to Invest in Your Back Yard as a Passive Investor

Your local or regional investment options are not limited to publicly traded companies either. There is a wealth of different ways to invest in your local economy and improve your investment returns.

Take the case of Daryl G. Durheim. Durheim had to look no further than his employer's business in metropolitan Minneapolis, Minnesota to find a suitable investment. The company had grown from the early 1900s as an architectural and engineering firm into a vertically integrated company encompassing the additional facets of construction and real estate development to its corporate mix. The strategy worked as the real estate development arm of the firm generated projects and income for its sister companies in the architecture, engineering, and construction segments of the business.

Then came the 1980s downturn in the real estate market, with a consequent reversal in the fortunes of the real estate development sector. Real estate operations started generating losses, tying up significant sums of money, and no longer feeding project generating revenues. The parent company made the painful decision to pull out of the real estate development/ownership business in 1984.

With the departure of the president of the real estate development company, Durheim was elevated to fill that position with the express directive from corporate management to extricate the company from existing real estate development projects and liquidate real estate ownership. By the summer of 1986, only the property management group remained of the real estate development company.

At this point, Durheim approached corporate management about their intentions to stay in the property management business and, if not, would they consider selling the business to him? It was a win/win situation for both parties.

Consider the facts. The company wanted to get back to the basics of the original company mission (architecture and engineering). No one at corporate really understood the property management business. At current operating levels, the property management business generated only enough to cover the personnel and administrative expenses. In other words, there was no return on the company's investment of financial and human resources. Simply put, the property management group no longer fit the corporate strategy for the future and was a drag on earnings and company resources.

From Durheim's perspective, he saw tremendous opportunity. An experienced staff was already in place to run operations. An existing customer base eliminated the need for substantial start-up costs. Office space could be negotiated at an attractive price from corporate. He was also convinced that he could eliminate many of the bureaucratic inefficiencies developed over the years. Equally important, he knew he could build an espirit de corps to eke out even greater operating efficiencies.

Most important of all, his in-depth understanding of the property management operation meant that he clearly understood the risks and potential of the business. No mistakes would be made on his part in negotiating the purchase price of the business.

Finally, Durheim had some leverage. If the company tried to sell the business outright to a third party, it ran the risk of losing valuable people as the pending sales became known. In addition, the loss position could worsen as time dragged on. It also faced severance pay and unemployment costs if a buyer could not be found and the operation had to be shut down.

"It all boils down to a matter of perception. Where the company perceived losses and risk, I perceived opportunity. Where the company perceived a lack of financial return, I perceived a financial livelihood and a chance to capitalize on my industry experience and knowledge and make an investment grow and secure our financial future," says Durheim, President of Appletree Properties, Inc. in Bloomington, Minnesota.

Two years after taking over ownership, Durheim and team guided the firm to a better than 60 percent increase in revenues and more than twice the square footage under management with little increase in staff size. Since then, cyclical market conditions have resulted in some shrinkage, but the business continues to provide Durheim with the financial security and personal satisfaction he sought when purchasing the business.

The Franchise Option

One way that many investors take a stake in their home community is by purchasing a franchise. Franchises offer a number of significant advantages over investing in venture capital projects. First, the franchisor has already performed the due diligence required to help ensure that the business will be a success. The company will have already performed the time-consuming and costly up-front business evaluation work such as market studies, facility layout, inventory and equipment requirements, and start-up and working capital levels.

Checking out the franchise route can help you avoid some costly mistakes. For example, you may be considering opening up a McDonald's-type fast food restaurant in your town with a population of 5000. McDonald's Corporation has already spent millions of dollars on market research and has pinpointed the population size, income level, other demographics, and level of existing competition that makes a town a candidate for success. Unless your town meets those criteria, your chances for success are slim to none. Remember, the brutal facts show that 20 percent of new businesses fail before the end of the third year. In comparison, top-quality franchises fail less than 5 percent of the time. Purchasing a franchise can help improve those odds, if you do your homework.

There are some tools to help you find the best franchise operation for you and your market. Just as public companies must provide potential investors with a prospectus, franchisors must provide potential franchisees with a copy of the franchise disclosure statement (Uniform Franchise Offering Circular). Make sure you take the time to read and thoroughly understand it. It's your best defense against purchasing the wrong franchise. Also, it sets out the obligations of the franchisor to you, the franchisee.

The disclosure statement contains plenty of useful information on the franchisor and its product or service. It will detail any problem areas such as pending or past suits against the franchisor (and some franchisors have notoriously been less than fair with its franchisees) or bankruptcies. Important financial information includes franchise fees, royalties, the franchisee's required initial investment, estimated working capital needs, and estimated expenses.

Pay particular attention to franchisor and franchisee obligations, specific restrictions (such as having to purchase all supplies from the franchisor), and reasons for and the process of possible franchise termination. Another key area is the discussion of market territory. Are you purchasing an exclusive territory, or can the franchisor sell another franchise two blocks down the street to compete with your business? There's no substitute for studying the disclosure statement thoroughly and getting independent legal or other types of expert advice.

Once you have read the disclosure statement and are still interested in the franchise approach, request earnings information of existing franchisees and a list of franchisee contacts. Call them to discuss how satisfied they are with the franchisor and how well their actual revenues and earnings match up with the franchisor's marketing claims or their anticipated return on investment.

Take one step further and personally visit other franchise operations that are not on the provided list to obtain an objective view of the franchise from the franchise owner. Ask about the pluses and minuses of the franchise. Inquire about any difficulties franchisees have had and what they would have done differently now that they have some experience in the business.

During this evaluation process, make sure you compare apples with apples. A franchise in booming Boise, Idaho may provide five times the revenues and earnings potential than one in a similar size Northeast community still undergoing economic stagnation. Seek out financial and market information on franchises as comparable as possible to your anticipated territory.

Finally, you must analyze your own experience, business skills, and temperament. Face it, some people are not cut out to run a business or deal with the public on a continuing basis. From the operations perspective, make sure you can have a qualified manager ready to run the business so that you don't have to spend the 12- to 16-hour days that it may require to get a business up and running.

Nail down the entire costs of running the business as close as possible. Don't forget to include such items as business license fees, insurance (property, liability, motor vehicle, etc.), business taxes such as property taxes (which in some states also get applied to inventory), utilities, and telephone. Then make up projected financial statements based on several different levels of operation including a breakeven analysis.

Make up a worst-case scenario and how you would cope with it. It is crucial to accompany these income and expense projections with a cash flow analysis to see where you might get into a cash bind. This way you can arrange for the required outside financing or bank credit lines to carry you through those cash droughts.

Inquire about the level of training your staff will receive. Is the training included in the franchise fee, or will you have to pay extra for it? In addition, what technical or franchisor staff support can your business expect? Does the franchisor provide free advertising materials or television or radio spots? Or are there cooperative advertising funds?

For additional information about franchises and informative brochures on franchises, the franchise industry, and franchise consultants contact:

American Association of Franchisees and Dealers
P.O. Box 81887
San Diego, CA 92138
800-733-9858

International Franchise Association/Franchise World Magazine
1359 New York Avenue NW, Suite 900
Washington, DC 20005
202-628-8000

Women in Franchising (training and consulting)
53 West Jackson Boulevard, Suite 205
Chicago, IL 60604
312-431-1467

Or find a copy of:

Franchise Opportunities Handbook
U.S. Department of Commerce
Washington, DC 20230

The Ratings Guide to Franchises
Facts on File
460 Park Avenue South
New York, NY 10016
212-683-2244

The Source Book of Franchise Opportunities
Robert E. & Jeffrey M. Bond
Irwin Professional Publishing
Burr Ridge, IL 60521

Worldwide Franchise Directory
Gale Research, Inc.
835 Penobscot Building
Detroit, MI 48226
800-877-4253

Buying Direct

Purchasing an existing business as an investment requires its own set of analysis parameters. Some variables to consider include:

- What is the reputation of the current business and owner?
- What are the underlying economic fundamentals of the industry?
- Who are your major customers (any recent changes in customer makeup?)
- Who are the major competitors?
- What competitive edge will you have?
- Who are the major suppliers?
- What market niche will you serve (discount/up-scale)?
- What products and services will you provide?
- Will key staff personnel/management stay after you purchase?
- What technical knowledge or other specialized expertise is required?
- How is the regulatory environment?
- How well maintained is the equipment?

- What arrangements are made for the premises (short-term or long-term lease, purchase, etc.)?
- Are you comfortable with the accuracy and detail of the financial statements?
- Have you made a realistic projection of future revenues and earnings?
- How will you verify the business valuation?
- Is seller financing available?
- What other financing options are available?
- What cash flows will be needed to keep the business operating smoothly?
- How much capital will be required to purchase the business and fund working capital?
- Did you get a noncompete clause in the contract?

Once you have satisfactory answers to all these questions, it's time to prepare a comprehensive business plan. This serves three major purposes.

1. It makes sure you have not forgotten to consider any critical element for the success of the business.
2. It provides you with the economic facts to determine whether this business venture can deliver the investment return you desire.
3. The business plan will play a major role in your efforts to obtain financing to purchase the business.

There are many excellent books and software programs to help you prepare a solid business plan. Pay particular attention to the industry, management, marketing, financial projections, and competitor sections. Much of the information can be gleaned from the work you did to provide answers to the questions listed above.

Eric Grushkin, a former investment banker and partner in Greg Partners in Cypress, California offers a word of caution: "If you plan to raise $1 million or more to purchase or start a business, you need to have a professionally prepared business plan designed for the particular audience in mind."

For in-depth information on various business valuation techniques, I recommend the following books:

- *Handbook of Business Valuation* by Thomas L. West and Jeffrey D. Jones, editors (John Wiley & Sons, 1992).
- *Valuing Small Business and Professional Practices* by Shannon Pratt (Business One Irwin, 1993).

If you don't possess the expertise to perform an accurate appraisal yourself, it's wise to pay for an independent appraisal by a firm familiar with the type of business you are purchasing.

Sometimes the appraisal service is part of a package of services available to the business buyer. For example, Business Team in San Jose and other California locations offers business search activities to help you find the business you want to buy, and then it helps you develop a pricing strategy and assists you in negotiations if you so desire. After your acquisition, Business Team offers a business buyer's protection plan, business consultation, and legal/accounting consultation to aid you in running your business.

The hometown investment arena offers substantial opportunities for the serious investor willing to take the time to develop important contacts, track the economic environment, and analyze the prospects of potential investment candidates. Invest in your backyard and reap the benefits.

Glossary

Accreted. The process of earning or growing gradually. For example, the interest on zero coupon bonds is accreted.

Adjustable rate preferred. A preferred security with its dividend payment pegged to a specific index or indices.

American depositary receipt (ADR). A negotiable receipt for shares of a foreign corporation held in the vault of a United States depositary bank.

Angel. An individual who provides venture capital to a start-up or expanding business.

Annual report. The Securities and Exchange Commisssion–required report presenting a portrayal of the company's operations and financial position. It includes a balance sheet, income statement, statement of cash flows, description of company operations, management discussion of company financial condition and operating results, and any events that materially impact the company.

Asset allocation. Investment strategy of reducing risk and increasing return by investing in a variety of asset types.

Asset play. A stock investment that value investors find attractive due to asset undervaluation by the market.

At the money. The situation when the underlying security's market price equals the exercise price.

Basis price. The cost of an investment used to determine capital gains or losses.

Bear market. A period of time during which stock prices decline over a period of months or years.

Bond. A long-term debt security that obligates the issuer to pay interest and repay the principal. The holder does not have any ownership rights in the issuer.

Bond ratio. The measure of a company's leverage comparing the firm's debt to total capital.

Bottom-up investing. Investment strategy starting with company fundamentals and then moving to the overall economic and investment environment.

Busted. A convertible whose underlying common stock value has fallen so low that the convertible provision no longer holds any value.

Call option. A contract providing the holder the right to buy the underlying security at a specific price during a specified time period.

Call provision. A provision allowing the security issuer to recall the security before maturity.

Cash equivalent. An asset type with maturities of less than one year.

Cash flow. The flow of funds into and out of an operating business. Normally calculated as net income plus depreciation and other noncash items.

Cash flow/debt ratio. The relationship of free cash flow to total long-term indebtedness. This ratio is helpful in tracking a firm's ability to meet scheduled debt and interest payment requirements.

Cash flow/interest ratio. How many times free cash flow will cover fixed interest payments on long-term debt.

Cash flow per share. The amount earned before deduction for depreciation and other charges not involving the outlay of cash.

Cash ratio. Used to measure liquidity. It is calculated as the sum of cash and marketable securities divided by current liabilities. It indicates how well a company can meet current liabilities.

Closed-end fund. An investment fund, with a fixed number of shares outstanding, that trades on exchanges like stock in regular companies.

Cluster investing. Method of diversification recommending investing in stocks from different clusters or groups.

Common and preferred cash flow coverage ratios. How many times annual free cash flow will cover common and preferred cash dividend payments.

Common stock ratio. The relationship of common stock to total company capitalization.

Contrarian. An investor seeking securities out of favor with other investors.

Convertible. A security that is exchangeable into common stock at the option of the holder under specified terms and conditions.

Covered call. An option in which the investor owns the underlying security.

Cumulative. As it relates to preferred stock, any unpaid preferred dividends accrue and must be paid prior to resumption of common stock dividends.

Current ratio. A liquidity ratio calculated by dividing current assets by current liabilities.

Cycles. Repeating patterns of business, economic, and market activity.

Cyclical. Industries and companies that advance and decline in relation to the changes in the overall economic environment.

Debt-to-equity ratio. The relationship of debt to shareholder's equity in a firm's capitalization structure.

Defensive investments. Securities that are less affected by economic contractions, thus offering downside price protection.

Diversification. The spreading of investment risk by owning different types of securities, investments in different geographical markets, etc.

Dollar cost averaging. Investment strategy of investing a fixed amount of money over time to achieve a lower average security purchase price.

Dow Jones Industrial Average. Market index consisting of 30 U.S. industrial companies. Used as a measure of market performance.

Dow theory. Investment theory that the market moves in three simultaneous movements, which help forecast the direction of the economy and the market.

Drip. Dividend reinvestment plan in which stockholders can purchase additional shares with dividends and/or cash.

Earnings per share. Net after-tax income divided by the number of outstanding company shares.

Economic series. The complete cycle of types of economic periods, such as from expansion to slowdown to contraction to recession/depression to increased activity back to expansion.

Economic value. With respect to stock, the anticipated free cash flow the company will generate over a period of time, discounted by the weighted cost of a company's capital.

Efficient market. A market that instantly takes into account all known financial information and reflects it in the security's price.

Exercise price. The price at which an option of futures contract can be executed. Also known as the striking price.

Expiration date. The last day on which an option or future can be exercised.

Federal Reserve. The national banking system consisting of 12 independent federal reserve banks in Atlanta, Boston, Chicago, Cleveland, Dallas, Kansas City, Minneapolis, New York, Philadelphia, Richmond, St. Louis, and San Francisco.

Fiscal year. The 12-month accounting period that conforms to the company's natural operating cycle versus the calendar year.

Freddie Mac. The nickname of the Federal Home Loan Mortgage Corporation.

Free cash flow. Determined by calculating operating earnings after taxes and then adding depreciation and other noncash expenses, less capital expenditures and increases in working capital.

Free cash flow/earnings ratio. The percentage of earnings actually available in cash. It is the percentage of free cash available to company management for investments, acquisitions, plant construction, dividends, etc.

Fundamental analysis. Investment strategy focusing on the intrinsic value of the company as evidenced by a review of the balance sheet, income statement, cash flow, operating performance, etc.

Gap. A trading pattern when the price range from one day does not overlap the previous day's price range.

Global depositary receipt (GDR). Similar to ADR. Depositary receipt issued in the international community representing shares in a foreign company. Other designations include international depositary receipt (IDR) and European depositary receipt (EDR).

Growth investments. Companies or industries with earnings projected to outpace the market consistently over the long term.

High-tech stock. Securities of firms in high-technology industries such as biotechnology, computers, electronics, lasers, medical devices, and robotics.

Hometown investment. An investment opportunity in the area in which you live.

Hybrid security. A security that possesses the characteristics of both a stock and a bond, such as a convertible bond.

Indenture. The legal contract spelling out the terms and conditions between the issuer and bondholders.

Index. Compilation of performance for specific groupings of stocks or mutual funds, such as the Dow Jones Industrial Average, S&P 500, etc.

Indicator. A measurement of the economy or securities markets used by economists and investment analysts to predict future economic and financial moves and direction. Indicators are classified as leading, coincidental, or lagging. Indicator examples include interest rate changes, utility consumption, number of unemployment claims, etc.

IPO (initial public offering). The first public offering of a company's stock.

Insider. Anyone having access to material corporate information. Most frequently used to refer to company officers, directors, and top management.

Institutional investor. Investor organizations, such as pension funds and money managers, who trade large volumes of securities.

In the money. The situation when the price of the underlying security is above the exercise price.

Intrinsic value. The difference between the current market price of the underlying security and the striking price of a related option.

Junk bond. A bond with ratings below investment grade.

Laddering. The process of purchasing bonds with different maturity dates in order to avoid reinvestment risk.

Leading indicator. An economic measurement that tends to accurately predict the future direction of the economy or stock market.

Leaps. Long-term equity participation securities. Long-term options with maturities up to two years.

Leverage. The use of debt to finance a company's operations. Also, the use of debt by investors to increase the return on investment from securities transactions.

Life cycle investing. Developing an investment strategy based on where you are in your life cycle.

Liquidity. The degree of ease in which assets can be turned into readily available cash.

Listed. Investment securities that have met the listing requirements of a particular exchange.

Maintenance margin. The minimum equity value that must be maintained in a margin account. Initial margin requirements include a minimum deposit of $2000 before any credit can be extended. Currently, Regulation T rules require maintenance margin equal at least 50 percent of the market value of the margined positions.

Margin. The capital (in cash or securities) that an investor deposits with a broker to borrow additional funds to purchase securities.

Margin call. A demand from a broker for additional cash or securities as collateral to bring the margin account back within maintenance limits.

Municipal bond. A bond issued by a local or state government or government agency.

Mutual fund. An investment company that sells shares in itself to the investing public and uses the proceeds to purchase individual securities.

NAFTA. North American Free Trade Agreement.

Naked option. An option written when the investor does not have a position in the underlying security.

NASDAQ. National Association of Securities Dealers Automated Quotation System, providing computerized quotes of market makers for stocks traded over the counter.

Net asset value (NAV). The quoted market value of a mutual fund share. Determined by dividing the closing market value of all securities owned by the mutual fund plus all other assets and liabilities by the total number of shares outstanding.

Numismatics. Study of, collecting, and investing in currency and metals.

OPEC. Organization of Petroleum Exporting Countries.

Obsolete security. Security that is no longer actively traded on an exchange but has collector value.

Option. A security that gives the holder the right to purchase or sell a particular investment at a fixed price for a specified period of time.

Out of the money. A call option whose striking price is higher than the underlying security's current market price; a put option whose striking price is lower than the current market price.

Participating. As it relates to preferred stock, the preferred stockholder shares in additional dividends as the earnings of the company improve.

Payout ratio. The percentage of a company's profit paid out in cash dividends.

Portfolio. The investment holdings of an individual or institutional investor, including stocks, bonds, options, money market accounts, etc.

Preferred. A security with preference to dividends and a claim to corporate assets over common stock.

Price/earnings ratio. Determined by dividing the stock's market price by its earnings per common share. Used as an indicator of company performance and in comparison with other stock investments and the overall market.

Private placement. The placement of a security directly with a person, business, or other entity without any offering to the general investing public.

Put option. A contract giving the holder the right to sell the underlying security at a specific price over a specified time frame.

Quick ratio. Current assets less inventory divided by current liabilities. Used to measure corporate liquidity, it is regarded as an improvement over the current ratio, which includes the usually not very liquid inventory.

REIT. Real Estate Investment Trust.

Range. The high and low prices over which the security trades during a specific time frame—day, month, 52-weeks, etc.

Rating. Independent ranking of a security in regard to risk and ability to meet payment obligations.

Rebalancing. The process of adjusting a portfolio mix to return to a desired asset allocation level.

Relative strength. Comparison of a security's earnings or stock price strength in relation to other investments or indices.

Risk. The financial uncertainty that the actual return will vary from the expected return. Risk factors include inflation, deflation, interest rate risk, market risk, liquidity, default, etc.

Rule of eight. Diversification strategy that contends a minimum of eight stocks is necessary to properly diversify a portfolio.

Secondary market. Market where previously issued securities trade such as the New York Stock Exchange.

Short against the box. Investment strategy of selling a security short while holding a long position in it.

Short sale. Sale of a security not yet owned to capitalize on an anticipated market price drop.

Short squeeze. Rapid price rise forcing investors to cover their short positions. This drives the security price up even higher, often squeezing even more short investors.

Special situation. An undervalued security with special circumstances such as management change, new product, technological breakthrough, etc., favoring its return to better operating performance and higher prices.

Spinoff. Shedding of a corporate subsidiary, division, or other operation through the issuance of shares in the new corporate entity.

Split. A change in the number of outstanding shares through board of directors' action. Shareholder's equity remains the same; each shareholder receives the new stock in proportion to his or her holdings on the date of record. Dividends and earnings per share are adjusted to reflect the stock split.

S&P 500. A broad-based stock index composed of 400 industrial, 40 financial, 40 utility, and 20 transportation stocks.

Striking price. The price at which an option or future contract can be executed according to the terms of the contract. Also called exercise price.

10-K, 10-Q. Annual and quarterly reports required by the Securities and Exchange Commission. They contain more in-depth financial and operating information than the annual and quarterly stockholders' reports.

Technical analysis. Investment strategy that focuses on market and stock price patterns.

Top-down investing. Investment strategy starting with the overall economic scenario and then moving downward to consider industry and individual company investments.

Total return. The return achieved by combining both the dividend/interest and capital appreciation earned on an investment.

Trading range. The spread between the high and low prices for a given period.

Turnaround. A positive change in the fortunes of a company or industry. Turnarounds occur for a variety of reasons such as economic upturn, new management, new product lines, strategic acquisition, etc.

Underlying security. The security that may be bought or sold under the terms of an option agreement, warrant, etc.

Undervalued situation. A security with a market value that does not fully value its potential or the true value of the company.

Underwrite. The effort by investment bankers to get investors to subscribe to an offering.

Uptrend. Upward movement in the market price of a stock.

Venture capital. Funds provided by individuals or businesses, as start-up or expansion capital for businesses, typically for an ownership percentage of the firm.

Volume. The number of units of a security traded during a given time frame.

Warrant. An option to purchase a stated number of shares at a specified price within a specific time frame. Warrants are typically offered as sweeteners to enhance the marketability of stock or debt issues.

Working capital. The difference between current assets and current liabilities.

Yield. An investment's return on investment from its interest or dividend-paying capability.

Zero coupon. A bond selling at a discount to maturity value and earning interest over the life of the bond but paying it upon maturity.

Index

About the Author

Richard J. Maturi is a widely respected business and investment author whose nearly 1000 articles have appeared in such distinguished publications as *Barron's, Investor's Business Daily, Institutional Investor, Your Money, Industry Week, Kiplinger's Personal Finance, The New York Times, Your Company,* and many others. He also publishes three investment newsletters, *Utility and Energy Portfolio, Gaming and Investments Quarterly,* and *21st Century Investments* (see coupon offer in the back of this book). His previous books include *The 105 Best Investments for the 21st Century* (McGraw-Hill, 1995), *Stock Picking* (McGraw-Hill, 1993), *Divining the Dow, Wall Street Words,* and *Main Street Beats Wall Street.*

Maturi is a member of the Society of American Business Editors and Writers, the American Society of Journalists and Authors, the Denver Press Club, and Wyoming Media Professionals. He and his wife, Mary, live in a log home in the Laramie Range of Wyoming's Rockies.